Travels with my Sketchbook

village outside Moscow

Travels with my Sketchbook

*A journey through Russia, Poland
Hungary and Czechoslovakia*

Nicholas Garland

HARRAP
London

First published in Great Birtain 1987
by Harrap Ltd
19-23 Ludgate Hill, London EC4M 7PD

© Nicholas Garland 1987

ISBN 0 245–54528–X

Designed by Gwyn Lewis
Phototypeset by Falcon Graphic Art Ltd
Wallington, Surrey
Printed and bound by
Mackays of Chatham Limited

The publishers and the author would like to thank
The Daily Telegraph for permission to publish material
contained in this volume written while the author was
a staff member of that paper.

CONTENTS

To Harry

INTRODUCTION

Some time in 1981 I went to see Bill Deedes, who was then Editor of *The Daily Telegraph*, where I worked. I had prepared a number of arguments in favour of the paper helping me to indulge a sudden impulse to travel.

I put it to him that, as a political cartoonist, I had to comment on news and events from all over the world yet I had never visited the Soviet Union or any Third World country. I had never set foot in India or China, or even been back to New Zealand where I had been brought up and which I had left nearly thirty years before.

I was ready to develop this theme but the Editor was already ahead of me. He waved my words aside and said: 'Of course you should travel. Fix up a trip and let me know where you want to go. Quite essential for your work, yes, yes . . . .' The interview was over, except that as I left the room he called after me the splendid phrase: 'Ventilate your mind!'

I chose to visit the Soviet Union first. I had already seen some of the USA and the other super-power seemed the obvious place to go. I had romantic notions of visiting Chekhov's homeland, and there is something about moody, emotional Russians that has always appealed to me. But what really clinched it was Harry.

He is a childhood friend of my wife, and for fifteen years he had been telling me I should visit the USSR. He has travelled widely behind the Iron Curtain for both work and pleasure, but Russia and Russians have a special attraction for him. A friend of ours said: 'Russia is an erogenous zone for Harry.'

He speaks the language fluently. When I asked him how good his Russian was he replied: 'Russians think I am a fellow-countryman, but they can't quite work out where I come from.' He is equally at home in German and French and he speaks Polish and some Czech too. He even learnt quite a bit of Hungarian before he went there.

Harry is an accountant by profession and an excellent amateur violinist. He lives in Vienna with his wife and son and is something of a mystery to even his closest friends. He is the same age as me, tall and strongly built. He dresses carefully, loves good food and wine, and as far as I know is more or less fearless.

Harry is not his real name. He prefers not to be identified, so I call him Harry after Harry Lime. Not because he is a villain. When a character in *The Third Man* is asked to talk about Harry Lime he replies: 'It's difficult. You knew Harry; we didn't do anything terribly amusing — he just made it all seem such fun.' Well, that's a pretty good description of this Harry too.

Anyway, as soon as I suggested a trip he planned it all and told me to fly to Helsinki and take a train to meet him in Leningrad, which I did. And as soon as our journey was over he pestered me to come with him to some other Communist states in order that he could teach me more about the system. As he said: 'Communism develops differently in different countries.' That's how a few years later we found ourselves in Hungary and Czechoslovakia.

During all the trips that I was given by *The Telegraph* I kept illustrated journals. They were written as sort of extended letters to my wife Caroline, and *The Sunday Telegraph* published extracts from several of them. Collected together here are the journals I wrote in Russia, Poland, Hungary and Czechoslovakia.

As I said, I flew to Helsinki . . .

RUSSIA

Wednesday 7 October 1981 (Helsinki)

. . . To continue: it was raining heavily when I got to the station. It gave one a big kick to see on the departures board '12.00 LENINGRAD ЛЕНИНГРАД 6'. Platform 6 was empty. I had been told to arrive half an hour before 12.00 but it was only 11.15 a.m. I sat down and waited. Next time I looked a beautiful green train was occupying quay 6. I thought I might as well get on it, and went out into the driving rain across the open platform and to the train. I tried the door of my wagon; it was locked. A woman gazed expressionless at me as I walked up to the next door. Also locked. I swore. I was wet. I walked back through the puddles past the woman in the window to the station. I found the Russian ticket office. Two Russians looking like cartoon Russians were talking to the woman at the desk. They smiled at something one of them said. I showed the lady my ticket. She turned it over, gave it back and said 'Yes'.

I said: 'Do I have to report to someone or just get on the train?' There was an instruction somewhere about meeting an Intourist official.

The lady did not understand. She said: 'Today — Number 6.'

'Now?' I said.

'Yes please.'

I went back to the door to platform 6. Through the rain the lovely green train stood deserted just as I had left it. I waited. Soon two men hurried out to the train, one reaching into a pocket as he went. I could see him quite clearly unlock the door and they both jumped in.

Encouraged, I set out once more through the downpour. They had left the door open. I got in. It is always surprising how high off the ground trains are. It was quite an effort to lift my bags up in front of me.

Inside, I know this sounds silly, but I was very struck by how cold it was. The air was cold, I swear it. I began banging my way down the corridor carrying my heavy grip in front of me.

Suddenly a uniformed woman appeared. She spoke in Russian but I heard, or thought I heard, the word 'billet' or something like it. I gave her my ticket. Behind her I could see the woman I'd seen before. She nodded and smiled at me now. Perhaps she was relishing the memory of me in the rain trying her locked doors — perhaps she was being friendly.

I was shown to a freezing compartment. It had two hard bunks. It was very clean and had a very convenient table — actually the flat cover of a sink. It also had a pillow and was not uncomfortable. I felt an enjoyable sensation of excitement sitting by myself in my compartment waiting to pull out. I had absolutely no sense of dread, just a delightful thrilled feeling as if I was saying to myself, as in a way I suppose I was, 'what an extraordinary thing for me to be doing'.

village seen from the Train

The horrible fear I had before the flight to Helsinki came from the certainty that if anything went wrong I would hit the ground at 500 miles an hour and be dead. The lack of it now was because if something went wrong now it would be an adventure and there would be every chance I would survive it.

When the train pulled out I stopped writing for a bit but I soon grew bored of looking at rain-swept birch and fir trees growing out of rocks and began to write again.

What really made me write was seeing a sign painted in white on the face of a cutting through the rock — I wanted to remember it. Some confused fool had drawn a CND sign with above it the word 'PEACE' and below it the word 'REVOLUTION', a somewhat sardine-toffee situation.

2.00 p.m.: We stopped on the outskirts of a small town. It had rained solidly so far. The landscape was dull and exactly what story books had led me to expect: fir trees, beeches, lakes, rocks. The occasional little wooden farm-house or hut could be glimpsed through the trees.

I had a good lunch and got a coffee from a lady with a trolley. She was pretty and smiled conspiratorily. A glum man pushed the trolley for her.

'Cream?' she said.
'Yes please.' She grinned.
'Sugar?'
'No thanks.' She beamed!

I meant to say I had found a switch for the heater, put it on to full, and the compartment was now warming up.

11

At about 3.45 p.m. the train stopped as far as I could see nowhere and some Russians came on board, wearing khaki uniforms with green caps or blue uniforms and caps.

I went and stood in the corridor to watch them as they took off raincoats and said hello to the female railway hostess.

A middle-aged Finn I had spoken to earlier watched them too. After a while he nodded to the drenched landscape outside.

'That was Finnish territory,' he said.

'Is it Russian now?' I asked. I seemed to remember there was a sort of no man's land between the two countries.

'Yes,' he said.

'Do you want it back?'

He grinned, thought for a bit and said,

'Well, maybe not me personally, but some of the older people.'

He said it formed one-fifth of the old Finland and the people who had lived there moved into Finland.

We had to stop chatting because a Russian official came and shut us into our compartments.

A few minutes previously two customs men or border guards had come in and taken away my passport.

They were unsmiling and suspicious looking but then customs men always are. One looked under my bunk with a torch and also up into the luggage-rack. God knows what they were looking for. You'd have to be a very brave and reckless smuggler to try to get anything through here.

Outside the window I could see some guards checking an empty goods train accompanied by a woman who was opening the sliding doors for them.

Two customs men just came in and examined my bags. One spoke a little English. He really went through my stuff. Opened my wash-bag, took out everything, felt round the inside of my grip. He made me empty my pockets, he turned out my wallet. He opened and flicked through all my books and then handed them over to his comrade to have a butcher's at them. As they were either Chekhov and Dostoevski, or Shakespeare and Dickens, I thought they'd be safe enough. Once or twice I smiled, surprised and amused at his thoroughness. He smiled too, but went right on, feeling round the lining of my raincoat.

He asked if I had friends in the Soviet Union and was I taking them presents.

I said I was meeting an Englishman who lived in Vienna and frequently visited the Soviet Union.

He asked over and over again: 'Have you any more money?'

Eventually he said: 'You can put your things back now.' I had to practically re-pack.

12

Then he searched me. His fingers lightly feeling for a money belt round my chest and waist. He patted my empty pockets and ran his hands down my legs and searched my ankles.

Thursday 8 October

I spent most of yesterday's (Wednesday's) train journey talking to a Finn, a salesman of machinery who travelled the USSR for half the year. He spoke Russian very well and was an interesting man full of information and advice. To summarize his view of Russia he said: 'I am always pleased and relieved to be out.' 'And sorry to go in?' I asked. He pondered and said: 'Well, it's my job — so in a way I cannot say I'm sorry to do my job.' 'Perhaps you mean you are glad to go home to your wife?' I suggested. 'I mean I am glad to be out,' he said, smiling. 'Perhaps you will understand in a few days' time.'

The time passed pleasantly. He went and ordered some tea and it came just as I had known it would from stories and films, in a tall glass in a metal holder with some little sweet biscuits.

As we slipped through the outskirts of Leningrad I pressed my nose to the window and stared and stared. Wet streets, a few cars, high-rise blocks of flats all lighted up. Not many people about. Here and there a much older building in a square perhaps. At the edge of the railway line the usual tangle of weeds and rusty metal, broken concrete and crumbling walls. I mean usual in the sense that British railway embankments look like that and so do French and Spanish.

Then the train stopped. I picked up my bags and got off the train. I looked for my travelling companion to say goodbye but he had vanished. A memory of getting off a ferry on my first visit to France came back. I was nineteen then and on my way to Paris. I felt the same kind of elation and schoolboy excitement — pure and delicious pleasure.

It had stopped raining and I set off to look for Harry, who had said he would meet me.

[As I wrote this at 9.00 a.m. I heard the clutter of horses hooves outside and saw a cavalcade of unmounted soldiers preceded by some small open carriages with more soldiers lolling in them. The horses pulling the little carriages had high arched collars and the whole scene was so classically Russian I could not believe it — a scene straight from Chekhov, the lazy languid officers in the carriages, the top-hatted coachmen, the straight lines of troops looking proud as horsemen always do . . . .]

Someone said 'Excuse me', and I saw a tall handsome young Euro-lad with a bit of paper in his hand. He was friendly . . . dressed in anorak and jeans and with any young man's 'cool'. He was in no hurry, made no conversation but was amiable and asked me to wait a moment.

We looked round the station in case Harry was waiting there. He wasn't so I was taken to a taxi.

I cannot, do not have time, to describe the delight I took in simply looking at the people — the trousers stuffed into boots, the caps, the high cheekbones, the squalor, the odd tousled haircuts, the padded jackets, the women's head scarves — all so expected and yet so extraordinary.

I remember that each time Caroline was pregnant we never somehow could begin to imagine the baby. We knew one was coming but it remained an abstract thought until suddenly there it was — a real baby that waved its arms and looked around and cried. My surprise and delight at being in Russia could not be compared with the arrival of the babies but there was something parallel in knowing what you were going to see and then being amazed and thrilled when you saw it.

The car shot off through empty streets, most of which after a while had the look of faded eighteenth-century grandeur. Very wide streets and old buildings with lovely façades, decorated windows, pillars and steps, most were pale coloured and very beautiful.

After five minutes or so of speedy driving we stopped at the hotel. I neither paid nor tipped the driver, uncertain about how to or whether Finnish money was acceptable.

I said thank you in Russian as my Finnish friend had taught me, and he replied 'Pozhaluista' as I had been told he would.

Two door men, elderly and uniformed, stared at me as I went through the revolving doors and stepped into an extraordinary world. This I had not been prepared for. It was dimly lit and yet twinkling with brass decorations set in shining marble, cut-glass light fittings, pillars and stairs, an eerie mixture of wonderful elegance charm and wealth, overlaid with decay. There was, for instance, a strong pungent smell in the air not horrible but vaguely unpleasant. In the end I thought it was like the smell of a baby's dirty nappy before the child had gone on to solid food. One of the doormen pointed to the reception desk where I signed in, handed over my passport and asked if Harry had arrived. 'No.' 'Is he expected?' 'I don't know.' The receptionist eventually said she'd ring my room and let me know but now she must deal with some more new arrivals. These gentlemen were waiting patiently behind me. One was Australian, the others English.

I went to my room and laughed out loud with delight. It was so absolutely wonderful. It was more like a suite. A large tiled bathroom and lavatory just inside the door, then down a passage to a spacious sitting-room with tables, a desk, chairs, sofa and wardrobe. On one wall hung a very bad nineteenth-century oil painting — a romantic landscape.

The bed was in a curtained alcove. I wandered about trying light switches, examining the empty refrigerator that stood uselessly in the passage. I lay on the bed, hung up my coat and decided to go and have a drink. Harry had said he'd meet me in the bar if we didn't see each other at the station.

I found the bar where I could only buy drinks with hard currency and chatted to two Canadians who were here on business. The Canadians said to me: 'If your friend does not arrive, don't worry. You will find things are more ordinary and familiar here than you think they will be. Simply ask for anything you want and go on and on until you get it. Sooner or later you will. Think of it like this — at home you live life at 50 or 60 miles an hour. Here you have to slow down to 15 to 20, that's all.'

After they left, with two whiskies inside me by then, I set·off to look for Harry again. At the reception the woman told me a Harry was here, he had arrived and she had twice called my room but I was not there. I thanked her and went to the restaurant. It was very crowded and a dozen couples were dancing at one end of the room to incredibly loud music. The air was stifling hot and sweating waiters pushed through the milling people. No one took the slightest notice of me. No waiter asked if I wanted a table. No diner could possibly have picked out one wandering, lost Englishman — the whole place was in an uproar. The music ended and a wave of dancers returning to their places hit me and I was pushed this way and that, not caring a bit. Harry may or may not have been there. I was already in a vaguely drunken, Russian mood of cheerfully not giving a damn about anything very much. I was half swept out of the restaurant back into the splendour and marble and relative quiet of the hotel lobby. There was Harry coming upstairs laughing and spreading his hands. 'Ah! There you are.' 'Boy! Am I glad to see you.'

We went straight to another smaller restaurant and sat down and immediately Harry began to show his extraordinary ability to make things happen.

He said: 'Let's have the lot — champagne, vodka and caviare, to start, and we'll see what else they've got.'

He called over a waiter who didn't come at once and when he did seemed to me to be saying 'Nyet' to everything Harry said to him. But eventually he brought some champagne.

'No,' said Harry, this is too sweet.'

'This is all we've got.'

'Try again.'

The waiter returned with some ice in a bowl and some bread. Soon he brought dry champagne, and caviare. Harry was charming the pants off him and his surly face broke into a grudging then a beaming grin. He came back with an ice bucket, a plate of smoked fish, and vodka.

15

'We're getting him organized,' said Harry. 'First the ice, then the bucket, then the caviare, now the vodka. He's all over the bloody place, but he's getting the hang of it.' He said something to a Russian sitting farther down the table who shrugged and half-smiled and said something back.

Harry laughed shortly. 'I said to him this is the first time an ice bucket has been brought out since Stalin died,' he said.

'You didn't,' I gasped. 'What did he say?'

'He said he didn't think that could be true.' Harry cackled and began talking to a pretty girl who was sitting next to him. She, it seemed, was a prostitute. Anyway she wanted his room number and asked if he'd like her to telephone later or tomorrow.

'Did you give it to her?'

'Yes.'

'Crumbs!'

'I'm interested to see what happens. Also I'd like to ask her if she works for the KGB.'

'Would she tell you?'

'She might — if I asked her at the right moment.'

Harry has a way of saying these outrageous things so very calmly and matter-of-factly — and he really means to do them — he is not kidding, his manner bends all the rules of conversation and behaviour. You can easily find yourself having the strangest conversations or doing the most unusual things, because with him they seem perfectly straightforward. It can cause complete strangers to become very intimate with him at once, or be overcome with embarrassment.

For example later that night we were walking far along the Nevsky Prospect. I saw a uniformed young man.

'Is he a soldier or a policeman?' I asked.

'Dunno,' said Harry. He walked up to the boy and spoke to him and the boy smiled slightly and replied. Harry spoke again. The young man was very embarrassed and turned away shyly still smiling and murmuring something.

Harry came back. 'He's a policeman,' he said.

'Why was he so embarrassed?'

'I don't know — just being spoken to by a foreigner perhaps.'

'Could he tell from your accent you are foreign?'

'I don't know, perhaps. I said to him "are you a policeman?" and he said "yes", so I said "I'm a stranger. Are you sure you are not a soldier?" ' Harry was half laughing — he had been teasing the young man for some reason.

'He said he was quite sure he was a policeman.'

The girl at the table was certainly behaving in the most straightfor-

wardly flirtatious way. She would catch my eye, pout slightly, lower her eyes, look up, smile. I was amazed. She was with another girl who was if anything prettier, but less active.

The meal was absolutely delicious and the vodka wonderful. The champagne was not too good — but it wasn't too bad either.

I was feeling wildly excited and happy. Harry was obviously enjoying himself too — particularly by speaking Russian and surprising the Russians either by his fluent command of their language or the weird things he said.

The atmosphere in this little restaurant was very hard to describe. I felt very strange not understanding a word of what was going on, and I had a strong sensation that the Russians, certainly the bad-tempered looking waiters, would not have been either friendly or helpful if I had been on my own. Yet as soon as Harry chatted them up for a moment or two a good natured, very relaxed friendliness appeared out of nowhere and I felt then accepted or welcomed in a peculiar, uncomplicated, warm-hearted way. I don't mean from the two prostitutes. They were all arch and affected and wanted money; but by all the others.

Harry suggested a walk and we left the hotel, turned right down Brodsky Street and immediately left. The night was mild — neither of us wore jerseys. We found ourselves on an extremely wide and handsome and almost empty street. There were shops with very little in them and they didn't have the huge shop windows we are used to in the West. A dress shop with perhaps two gowns in a window. A completely empty dairy shop, a window filled with a pyramid of tinned tomato juice.

'That must be what's in stock this week,' muttered Harry.

The pavement was rough and slightly puddly. The all-over effect was one I now associate with Leningrad — one of truly great beauty and splendour that had tragically been allowed to run down and become so seedy and battered that you felt tormented by the waste of it, and angry that it had not been possible to preserve.

'What do you think of the Nevsky Prospect?' said Harry.

'Is this the Nevsky Prospect?'

'Mm.'

I was once more thrilled — like a little boy. I felt like the Americans I saw in London excited by discovering they were near some spot described by Dickens. But London had changed so completely that frequently Americans must read a plaque which said: 'Here on this spot stood. . . .' But the outline — the proportions, the very buildings of the Nevsky Prospect were the same as when Gogol described them. No high-rise blocks dwarfed the magnificent street, no sheet-glass windows blindfolded the rich façades. no 'development' that I could see. Certainly not half drunk in the middle of the night anyway. Now and then a car passed or a lone pedestrian; otherwise the bustle and roar of the Nevsky Prospect was quite stilled. We crossed over the canals, saw a sign on the chipped plinth of a statue. The sign informed passers-by that the chips were caused by Fascist shelling during the war. As we walked on down this dream-like street, which stretched on and on like an everlasting stage set, grim reality began to break through the romance.

Dreadfully dirty telephone boxes leaned against the walls here and there in little clusters. Some were lit, some not. Some had doors, some didn't; now and then a door squealed and rattled in the slight wind — the sort of detail that in a film prepared one for an unpleasant shock. There were mineral-water vending machines that looked more as if they dispensed cholera. 'Place 2 copecks in slot and sprint to the nearest lavatory.' Some machines had dirty glasses lying around on top. I thought people had left their disposable glasses there instead of in the bin provided. But there was no bin provided and anyway they were the glasses you drank from. Some had no drinking vessels at all and looked so filthy and uninviting you couldn't believe anyone would use them, although the next day I saw them in use.

I stopped by a bit of paper pasted on to a drain-pipe. On it was written this message that Harry translated for me:

A FAMILY WITH TWO-YEAR-OLD DAUGHTER WILL RENT A SEPARATE FLAT — VERY URGENTLY NEEDED. THE FAMILY DOESN'T NEED POLICE REGISTRATION FOR LENINGRAD

Below this message the paper was cut into easily torn off strips each with the same phone number written on it. It was such a desperate little note one felt touched by the unknown story that must lie behind it.

I wanted to peel off the note as a souvenir, but even though it looked pretty old and one phone number had been torn off, we decided we'd leave it it case it might yet produce a flat for the family.

I looked through an archway that led to a yard.

'I wonder what's in here?' I asked. 'Dunno — flats probably,' said Harry marching boldly in. We came to a small yard — it was littered with rubble and refuse and dimly lit. Several padlocked doors led off it and one that was ajar. We went in and found ourselves at the foot of a once handsome panelled stone staircase. It was dirty now, the banisters were rickety, the walls were streaked and chipped, wires hung loosely from the wall, and pipes had been installed passing through holes fives times too big and never made good. The air reeked of urine and garbage. On the first landing a bucket stood full of rotting apple peel and eggshells.

'Apples must have been in this week,' murmured Harry.

We climbed the stairs marvelling, at least I was marvelling at the incredible squalor. Harry was making jokes about it. It is not that you couldn't find sights like this in England — of course you could and much much worse. But this was the Nevsky Prospect. This was Regent Street as it were or Pall Mall. On one door at the top of the house we counted six doorbells. I wondered briefly why I didn't feel I was trespassing or at least in some way invading someone's territory.

Harry explained: 'It's because it doesn't belong to anyone. It's the State's. No-one cares.'

From then on the crumbling walls outside, the pot-holes and the signs of decay began to loose their charm — and some remote, uncentred, vague sense of dismay and anger spoilt the hitherto pure enjoyment. Something awful had happened here — was still happening. Groping for a way of describing it to myself, it occurred to me that the whole thing was like a vast slow-motion accident that began eighty years ago and now the dented, bashed in, smashed and ruined end must be near. A horrible silence must soon fall and the stunned victims let go, open their eyes and look around and perhaps try to sit up. I am letting my metaphor run away with me. It's just that I had never seen anything like this — it was so puzzling, being so attracted to a place and a people that in some ways were so horrifying and repellent.

Our walk went on and on through the night. We entered several buildings, rode up in old, old lifts and walked down wide mucky stairs. In the midst of this poverty electric lights blazed and huge radiators warmed the balmy night air; energy didn't seem to be a problem, or time-switches and thermostats were not available.

[I am writing this sitting in the service bureau, waiting for my tickets to Moscow. A wonderful, elderly lady has just sat down near me and is roaring into the phone — she appears to be both annoyed and amused. She is very elegant and round her throat wears a gold brooch on a gold chain that she is playing with as she chuckles and chides. She looks so aristocratic and confident. She is so magnificent in her good-humoured aggressive way — I wonder where on earth (and how) she lives in this strange city. She certainly doesn't come from anywhere we visited that night of the Nevsky Prospect. When she got up to go she gave me a radiant smile, gave a huge shrug, dropped her hands to her lap in a gesture of comic despair and gave a great gurgling laugh. Then up she got and stormed out.]

Eventually we returned to the hotel. On the corner of Brodsky Street I heard the chink! chink! of hammers — we went to investigate. Sitting on a low wall on the pavement, part of the entrance to the metro, was a huge workman. He was wearing a dark, frayed padded jacket, and heavy working trousers and boots; on his head he wore a brightly coloured peaked cap. Near him worked a woman in her fifties dressed exactly the same apart from her head, on which she wore a neckerchief. They were repairing a wall. A lorry had bumped and cracked it.

'Why at 2.00 in the morning?' I asked. Harry laughed.

'Perhaps they want overtime.' Harry at once struck a conversation with them. It ranged from Solidarity . . .

THE LADY: 'Walenska wants to bring back capitalism . . .'

20

To my drawings . . .

THE LADY: 'He's made me look too fat.'

THE MAN: 'He's got me exactly.'

Harry gave the man an English cigarette and both workers knocked off for half an hour's chat.

The woman remembered the war and the blockade and was firm in her support of her Government. The man was charmingly sceptical — expected very little from anyone. The woman said everything would be OK so long as our countries did not go to war against each other. Harry gave the workman a packet of cigarettes. At first the man said no, but then accepted them quite graciously. Both of them were extremely relaxed, amused, polite and friendly although as we approached they had looked almost unbelievably grim.

The amount of progress they were making seemed incredibly slight — with hammers and coal chisels they were re-levelling a broken concrete wall. The man sat at his task, one foot carelessly crushing some geraniums growing in a small flower-box.

As we said goodnight the chink of their hammers sounded again.

Breakfast (Thursday morning) was another delight. Harry was already there when I arrived and he told me I should pay, then take or ask for whatever I wanted. Tea included or coffee extra.

The choice was enormous. Sausage, salami, cheeses, a kind of hot semolina with melted butter, several kinds of sweet bun or cake, pancakes, bread, butter, jam. That was just some of it. Lots of buttermilk, prune juice, very sour tomato juice, mineral water. There were several salads and dishes of stuff that I haven't the faintest idea how to describe — brown or yellow stodge of some sort. It was very good. I love breakfasts anyway and this was a good one.

At the service bureau we checked out theatres and plays. Harry chose a modern Russian play, I chose *Rigoletto*. Harry said the girl tried hard to persuade him not to go to the play . . . 'It's trivial rubbish, modern slice of life, silly.' Poor girl — all this merely whetted his already huge appetite.

We booked seats and then decided to go to see the Hermitage. It was comfortable walking distance from the hotel and we turned into The Nevsky Prospect, first checking the progress on the broken wall at the corner of Brodsky Street.

The top of the wall was not yet level or even, but the new slab of polished stone had been rested on top anyhow. The lower part of the wall was badly cracked and therefore there seemed very little point in starting repairs at the top. However that's what had been done.

The pavement was crowded with men and women, most of whom

walked very purposefully and jostled their way along with little thought for their fellow-citizens. One was constantly nudged and bumped, sometimes even from behind.

The crowd was drab — boringly rather than badly dressed. You saw many uniformed men mostly military, some police. The officers looked quite smart but the regular troops were poorly dressed and rather stupid. We were accosted many times by young men, mostly looking pretty tough, who asked to change money. Harry either said, 'fuck off' or its Russian equivalent, to them or asked their price to see how high they'd go. Then asked for twice as much. He said his interest was entirely academic — he had absolutely no inclination to start illegally trading in foreign currency with a KGB plant.

The architecture, which was splendid in the Nevsky Prospect, became majestic, breathtaking, by the Winter Palace. The size and scale of the great squares, arches, terraces and Palaces is difficult to describe. It simply wasn't like anything I had ever seen. For a start the buildings were the most lovely and unexpected colours — blue, yellow and off white — and there was barely any traffic to blur the edges and disturb one's senses. That traffic which did exist moved down the streets like charging rogue elephants — it was anyone's guess which way it might decide to go — and there was no reason to suppose the cold-blooded drivers would make the slightest effort to avoid you. We skirted the Winter Palace and looked over the Neva. I won't go on and on about it. It was just terrific. A huge river. An immense river, cold and impersonal. Not like the friendly, busy Thames or the romantic Seine — more like an ocean. On the far shore one could see other buildings and beyond them newer blocks and towers.

Before I came on this trip I never really believed I'd ever get to the Hermitage. I've known about it, heard travellers tales about it for years but I was not prepared for it all the same. Here the Russians have halted the dreadful decay that has so terribly affected so much of the city. The pictures are not always so easy to see because of where they are hung — sometimes against the light streaming in through the windows, sometimes too much in the light so their surface reflects the sunshine, but I can't really criticize the place or the collection.

We didn't see half of it I'm sure but I saw what I came for. First the Dutch paintings. Terborch, Metzu and Rembrandt. As we came to the end of the Rembrandt gallery a girl stepped up to Harry and shook hands. He didn't recognize her at first and then said, very surprised: 'Oh, it's the girl from last night.' He began an animated conversation in Russian. Her companion was standing nearby and came over to me. She smiled and said:

'I speak a little English.'

'Oh good,' I said. There was a pause. Harry and the dark girl were talking.

'These are wonderful pictures,' I said, feeling stupid and uncertain how much she could understand English.

'Yes,' she said smiling and looking at me closely. I felt quite horribly embarrassed and couldn't think what to say.

'I work in TV,' she said. 'I am studying.'

'Studying pictures?'

'Studying.'

'Oh.'

'Do you want me today?' she asked, smiling again.

'What?'

'Do you want me? Do you want me in your room?'

'Do I want you?' I said, looking desperately round for Harry who had his back to me. I called his name. I still wasn't certain whether she knew what she was saying. Perhaps her English was very bad and she wasn't suggesting what I thought she was suggesting. Her manner was odd, because she wasn't being particularly flirtatious or suggestive — she was being friendly and matter of fact.

'What is your room number?' ('Harry, turn round — come and help me,' I prayed.)

'I will not be in my room at 1.00.'

'Later?'

'No — not later, I don't know when. No, sorry.'

'Well — what is your room number? I will call you — come and see you.'

'No, no, thank you.'

24

We stood for what seemed hours not saying any more. Now and then I could sense she was looking at me but I was simply too flabbergasted to raise my eyes. I stared at the floor.

At last Harry ended his conversation. The two girls said 'goodbye' and turned away. And we went back into the gallery. Harry said his girl had not been quite so straightforward as the other. They had not made any arrangements to meet. He was considering, and rejecting, the possibility of them being agents of some sort following us. I said they couldn't be. He said: 'Of course they can be.' 'But how would they know we would be at the Hermitage?' 'Because they could have followed us or the hotel porter could have told them. After all, you asked him how to get here so *he* knew where we were.'

It was the strangest incident. I have been in art galleries in lots of countries. Wicked places such as New York, Chicago, Paris, Amsterdam, London, but I've never been approached like that before — my first gallery in staid and proper repressive and strict Russia and bang — well not bang actually but — I could hardly believe it. Harry was quite as fascinated as I was. We went to look at the French nineteenth- and twentieth-century rooms and I blew my mind on Cézanne, Degas, Van Gogh, Picasso and last of all Matisse. I could have stayed in those rooms for hours, but Harry wanted to go so we left. I was determined to go back on the Saturday morning before our departure.

In the afternoon we took a hydrofoil down the Neva to Peter the Great's Summer Palace. We arrived at about 4.30. Harry asked when the next boat was going back. 'This is the last boat going back' he was told. 'Oh Christ, how will we get home?' 'By train.' I was pleased — it would be a chance to see some countryside and suburbs. (You don't see much from the boat.)

To get to the hydrofoil station we took a bus. I had seen people getting on to buses. It is not quite the same as London. 'Right that's the lot, no standing, c'man, 'nuther one right behind,' etc. Leningraders fight and push their way on to buses until they are absolutely crammed, so full that the last few people on prevent the doors from shutting and the buses pull away with the doors open and with passengers desperately flailing around trying to gain a couple more inches to allow the doors to close behind them. Our bus wasn't quite that full but pretty nearly. We pushed our way in and stood jammed up with everyone else. You pay by giving five copecks to the person next to you who passes it on until it reaches someone near enough to a ticket machine (of which there are several down the length of the bus) who buys your ticket for you which is then handed back the same way. You have to fight just about as hard to get off — but it's downhill as it were, and therefore easier.

Peter's Summer Palace was very pretty and had a spectacular water garden before it decorated with many shining gold statues. They gleamed so brightly in the pale fitful sunshine that they had a surrealist and rather ridiculous look. The German army occupied the Palace during the blockade of Leningrad. When they left they burnt it to the ground, and carried away the statues from the garden. More or less everything you saw today was restored work. All the floors, all the plaster-work, most of the panelling, the doors and windows. It was very very impressive. With tremendous care, bit by bit, the whole ornate and magnificent Palace had been rebuilt. From surviving fragments of wall hangings more had been embroidered or printed, intricately carved panels had been made from the existing original drawings and so on. Only the paintings were the real thing — they were carried to safety before the Germans arrived.

Army officers in Peter's Summer Palace Leningrad

The effect was odd. It was very touching that it had been done so painstakingly and well and it all had a new bright look, so you saw an eighteenth-century building with no patina of time.

Here Harry struck up an acquaintance with two women, one about twenty-nine the other a little older. The older one, Vera, had her little boy of four with her. She was tall and well built, dark and beautiful, with heavy lidded eyes and a wide mouth. Her sister-in-law Tatiana was also tall and big, but she was blond and snub-nosed with an odd pouting lower lip. Both seemed to know an awful lot about the Palace, and it turned out that Vera, who was married to an officer in the navy, was brought up near the Palace and as a child she had played in the ruins. Later she trained to be a guide here but had never started work because she married. Tatiana was also married to a sailor, who was in Argentina at that moment. Harry talked non stop to them, occasionally translating the good bits to me. The best room was a chamber with the walls literally covered with 300 portraits, mostly of girls — serfs, Vera said, who were dressed up in fine clothes to pose for the artist.

Boys buying ice cream outside a railway station Leningrad

When the time came to leave Vera and Tatiana said they would show us where to get the bus to the train. Unknown to me the plan developed. At one stop Vera and her little son got off but Tatiana stayed with us. It turned out Harry had invited them all the way back to Leningrad for a drink. Vera had taken the boy to her mother's house and was going to meet us at the station. I was quite surprised at this arrangement, partly because both women were married and partly because Leningrad was about fifteen miles or so from where we were which seemed a long way to go for a drink. 'God no,' said Harry. 'For a drink, in an Intourist hotel, with two westerners? They'll dine out on this for years. They've probably never spoken to a westerner before.'

Newspaper & Journal kiosk
Peters castle station Leningrad

Once again Harry's ability to converse was marvellous to watch. I don't think it is any effort for him at all. All the way in, in the lovely old-fashioned train, Vera and Tatiana chattered away to him telling him about the blockade — 'now we are passing the spot in the suburbs which is the nearest the Fascists got to the city'. Encouraged by the success of this advance the commander of the German army cabled home to Hitler: 'We are in Leningrad.' It was their last advance and the city never fell. The two Russians also talked about the rows and rows of high-rise housing blocks we were passing. They looked pretty horrible to us but they were proud. 'All of them put up in five years!' they boasted. Tatiana also said she was on a waiting list for an apartment, and had been for five years. She had been told she'd have to wait another five years. I will be an old lady, she said. What looked ghastly to us was what she wanted more than anything.

Although these two very attractive and vivacious young women had by chance met two strange men and agreed to accompany them for a drink, and although they were extremely gay and merry, as far as I could see there was not the slightest kind of flirting or suggestion of any such possibility in their manner or talk. I asked Harry later about it and he said 'absolutely not — not at all. Russian women are different from western women in that way. They can take charge of a situation — direct it in the way they want to. They are much more powerful than their men as a rule. By chance they had got the opportunity of an unusual night out — they just wanted to have a good time — so they came with us.'

It was fun travelling through Leningrad with two Russians. They were so at ease, for instance, finding their way by metro (yes, spotlessly clean and efficient) that you felt being with them you were almost a Russian too. (Not that Russians were fooled — a boy told us the next day, 'I could tell you two were westerners 200 yards off'.) When we got to the street where the hotel was something odd happened. Harry walked on towards the hotel. Vera and Tatiana stopped on the other side of the road. I was caught in between as it were. I was puzzled and pointed to the hotel where Harry was going. They smiled and said something to me

Tatiana   H.   Vera

29

which they repeated. I ran after Harry calling to him. He looked round and went back towards them. They all spoke together for a few moments. Harry explained: 'They don't want to come to the hotel.' 'Why ever not?' 'It's an Intourist hotel. Full of foreigners. Russians are not supposed to go there, unless they are staying there. They feel uncomfortable about it.'

It was the first sight I've had of the system working. The first little glimpse of the sort of pressures a Russian citizen was under. Evidence of the huge gulf that there was between our system and theirs.

Harry managed to persuade them that it would be OK and, looking subdued and a bit embarrassed, they came in. We sat in a hard currency bar where roubles were not accepted. We could buy them champagne in their home town in a bar which they shouldn't be in, with money it was illegal for them to possess. It was stupid. They were not so cheerful it seemed to me in the bar — and I didn't enjoy it either. I gave Vera a packet of chewing-gum for her kid.

We had already booked a table at the Sadko Restaurant nearby and Harry changed it from three to four persons (he had been going to ask the mother of a friend of his,) and after a bit we walked over there. It was only fifty yards from the hotel. Here another weird scene occurred. We had been told that very loud music was played at the Sadko and we had asked to be put in the quietest place available. Harry asked the head waiter again to be put somewhere quiet because even outside in the lobby the noise was awful. The man grinned, shrugged and said 'there is your table'. It wasn't a quiet spot, but we had to accept it.

When we sat down it appeared there had been some mistake. The whole table was laid out with the most enormous feast. There were serving plates full of smoked salmon and other fish. There was caviare, meat and salad, vodka, a great jug of red wine and champagne in an ice bucket, black and white bread and numerous dishes of sauce and odds and ends. It looked absolutely fabulous, and would obviously cost the earth.

Harry called over the waiter and an argument commenced, with Harry at his most aristocratic and authorative. Other waiters came and listened. All this was shouted over the blaring trumpets, banging drums and horribly amplified guitars of the terrible groups.

'What are you saying?' I screamed. Harry leant across looking wicked: 'I said I ordered a table for four and I expect to see a menu. So you can take all this away and if you won't — call the manager.' He was having the time of his life. Vera and Tatiana calmly waited for things to get sorted out, Tatiana puffing on a cigarette, Vera raising her eyebrows and smiling at Harry's performance.

One waiter looking haggard appealed to me: 'Sprechen Sie deutsch?'

Sadko Restaurant

'Nein,' I replied 'Français or English — speak to him.' I pointed at
Harry. Then I gave up. The noise of the band, the champagne I'd
already drunk and the utter craziness of the situation produced in me a
feeling of bliss. I leaned back, ignored the whole lot of them and began
drawing the band. When I looked round again waiters were taking plates
away.

'We're getting them organized,' said Harry.

'What's going on,' I bellowed.

'Well,' yelled Harry, 'they say this is how they do things here, but
we've compromised and they've agreed to take half of it away.' He was
delighted.

The evening began to get muzzy from then on. Tatiana prepared the
caviare for us. She spread butter very thickly on bits of bread then
caviare on that. It was so delicious. Down went the smooth vodka — the
conversation got more and more excited, vehement and funny. People
began dancing. We began dancing. There was more champagne. A
Scotsman sang an awful song, unbelievably badly. Harry and I winced.
'What's the matter?' said Vera, 'People always sing in restaurants.' She

31

Sadko Restaurant Le...

asked me to dance; my head was swimming terribly from the drink and the heat but she laughed and whirled about. I tried to think — is this what the *Telegraph* wanted me to do here?

'What would your editor think of this?' asked Harry.

'He'd absolutely love it,' I said.

'Isn't it marvellous!' he said.

Vera asked me to do a drawing of our party as a little memento but I was far too drunk — so I did some caricatures of politicians instead. I could just about do that. Harry told her this was the sort of thing I published in my newspaper. I had done a picture of Mrs Thatcher like a schoolteacher wigging members of her Cabinet. Vera didn't say 'I don't believe it' — she said it was hard for her to understand it being tolerated.

Once, after dancing, we got back to the table and to my horror there was a new plate of smoked fish, more bread and a new jug of vodka waiting for us. I had not only drunk quite enough but I was also very full of food. Before I could express my dismay Harry said quickly: 'This is their donation to the evening, so eat it!' With profuse thanks and expression of great satisfaction we ate and drank it all — or most of it. I did think it was very nice of them, and it illustrated a little of the uncomplicated friendliness that they felt and expressed. When the bill came it was in two parts and we all put our money down together.

During the evening Tatiana told a little story. She went on a trip for some reason to Kiev. She arrived very late at the hotel and was told: 'There is no room'. She protested that she had booked the room before she left. 'No room.' An argument followed in which it emerged she hailed from Leningrad. 'You came from Leningrad?' 'Yes.' 'You are not a Muscovite?' 'No.' 'In that case, yes we do have a room, come in!'

All the time Vera and Tatiana talked about the war they never said 'The Germans'; they always talked about 'The Fascists'. They said they had no ill feeling against Germans. 'There are good and bad people in all countries. Russian soldiers behave very badly sometimes!'

At last we left the restaurant and someone suggested we went for a walk. It was about 11.45 p.m. and outside it was refreshingly cold and occasionally raining very slightly. The streets and squares were quite empty, and it was lovely walking along asking 'what is that building?' or 'what is that statue?' We passed a memorial to Pushkin. Vera led us to a red palace and told us a long rambling tale of murder and intrigue which resulted in the palace being unused for years and being known as the Castle of Blood. We saw the everlasting flame burning in memory of the Decembrists, and Tatiana explained that the flowers strewn around were left by young couples after their marriage. 'They come and leave flowers here or on the grave of those who died during the blockade,' she said.

We strolled by the Neva and back up Nevsky Prospect. We saw a sign painted in white and blue, also decorated with flowers. The sign read: 'Citizens — when the German artillery is shelling the city it is safer to walk on the other side of the street.'

As we walked along arm in arm up the Nevsky Prospect a young man emerged from nowhere and spoke to me — he wanted to change money. The two Russian women and Harry all spoke to him roughly: 'Clear off,' 'Get lost,' 'Go away.' A look of comic amazement crossed his face — he thought we must all be foreigners and couldn't cope with this chorus of Russian. Harry was highly amused at his discomfort. I think Vera and Tatiana were a bit embarrassed — ashamed perhaps of what they thought was the young man's brutishness.

We arrived back at Brodsky Street and I examined the broken wall again. No change. There were a number of taxis hanging around and Tatiana and Harry began haggling with various drivers to make the long journey out to Tatiana's mother's home. At first they all said 'No.' Harry said: 'I don't understand the system. If you go further you pay more — but they still say no.' He tried to bribe one driver with a five-dollar bill. No go. It was getting terribly late and cold by now, but neither Vera nor Tatiana seemed anxious — just bored at having to wait. And after a while — as they knew one would — one agreed to take them.

They shook hands, got in the car, waved and were gone.

Friday, 9 October

After breakfast I wanted to walk, simply to explore the streets and to look into shops and cars and so on. The obvious place to start was up The Nevsky Prospect, the wide straight street that runs a mile or so right through the heart of the city.

For a description of what it was once like read the first two pages of Gogol's story *The Nevsky Prospect*. It was because these lines had so impressed me when I first read them that I was excited to find myself there on my first night in the city.

'Nothing could be finer than Nevsky Prospect, at least not in St Petersburg; it is the be all and end all. It positively glows and sparkles — it is the jewel of our capital. . . .' That is not the impression it gives nowadays. Dilapidated, dirty and crumbling — its outline and generous proportions all intact but so uncared for.

The writers having breakfast.
Europiska Hotel Leningrad

34

a drunk reels by

All through the day the pavements were thickly crowded. If you stood on tiptoe, before you was a river of heads. Everyone seemed to be walking purposefully yet either they weren't going anywhere or they were being constantly replaced by more people. The crowd, in my fancy, seemed to be a single moving thing — aimless yet in a hurry. (Contradictory notions of this sort go through your mind the whole time here.)

We crossed the road; the traffic was sparse. Filthy buses and trolley buses and few speeding cars. Almost directly across The Prospect from our street was a very big department store. I suppose it was built in the early nineteenth century. There was an arched covered pavement along it's whole length, and one floor up there was another — like a great stone balcony. Inside it was a mass of small partitioned areas which in Gogol's day presumably housed stalls displaying goods. Now each area had a counter running across it so that you pointed to what you wanted from among the goods stacked on shelves out of your reach. No-one was allowed to handle goods here except in the clothes departments.

I like shopping in strange places very much — who doesn't. Everyone had told me: 'You will find nothing to buy,' but I knew I would — not in the tourist shops, or clothes, or luxury goods places but in little out-of-the-way stalls or hardware shops or, best of all, stationery stores.

Two things struck me immediately about this shop. Firstly, it was extremely crowded — really packed — like a last-minute Christmas rush in London, except that people had the same sort of aimless urgency about them — their faces were not animated — no one laughed or smiled as far as I could see; and, secondly, that the goods on sale, where there were any, were pitiful. Boring, dull, tacky, pathetic. Mighty Russia had produced one toy stall with three or four plastic toys of the kind you warn your children not to spend their pocket-money on because they will just break. Next to it another toy stall selling the same unusable things. I watched a woman folding socks, hideously patterned and apparently made out of cardboard. She had done several boxes and had a lot more to do.

'Imagine what it must do to you to be handling and selling this rubbish all day,' muttered Harry. It was an appalling idea — and he was quite right surely — it must destroy you.

We saw one of Russia's famous queues forming — suddenly the crowd in one place took on a shape as if a magnet had been thrust into iron filings and the line snaked away from a clothes stall, growing all the time. We tried to see what was being sold. It appeared to be bright green, flowered, overall-cum-housecoat garments. Presumably cotton, not nylon which made them special. The queuers were allowed into the 'shop' in little groups of four or five at a time, and a couple of assistants by the exit counter were wrapping the clothes in sheets of what looked like newsprint.

We saw other queues forming — one for fur hats — but I realized almost at once my friends had been right: there was absolutely nothing to buy. Not even if you contorted yourself nearly inside out and looked for something really horrible — it was all just boring gunk, mass-produced, cheap, dull rubbish. The only thing ghastly enough to catch my attention were some little statues made of silvery grey metal. They were of naked athletes or footballers and so awful I laughed at them; but they were very expensive and looked far too heavy to carry home as a joke. And anyway they were not funny — they were ugly.

In the end I bought some cotton because the cotton reels were made of wood. At home these days they are all plastic and you can't make tanks out of them and you can out of wooden ones.

Pushing through the crowd, we were constantly being accosted by young would-be money-changers. Harry asked one of them (having said 'No deal') what some queue was for and in no time, as is his way, they fell into conversation.

Sasha was twenty-five years old, slim and dark with almond eyes and the longest upper lip I've ever seen. It gave him an odd whacky expression and he had grown a small neat moustache, perhaps to disguise

Sasha

in some way his peculiar look. He carried a folding umbrella in his hand. He was very helpful and apparently quite frank but there was something off-putting about his sleepy eyes and depressed mien. He was full of information.

HARRY: 'We are told in the West never to change money illegally because you may find you are dealing with a KGB plant.'

SACHA: 'What nonsense — I'm twenty-five years old and I've never seen a KGB man. Anyway they wouldn't ask someone to change money just to trap them: they would be soliciting someone to commit a crime — and that is itself illegal.'

I expressed interest in the fact that the shops were so poorly stocked.

SACHA: 'There are more goods here in Leningrad than outside in small towns and villages. People have lots of money (he used an expression 'money in the sock') but there is nothing to spend it on.'

I asked how come on a Tuesday morning the streets and shops were so crowded — why weren't the people at work?

37

SACHA: 'They have come in from outside to do some shopping perhaps and people often take a little time off work to do some shopping and then return.' (He shrugged.)

I ASKED: 'Why aren't you at work?'

SASHA: I am a student and I have sometimes two or three days in the week when I do not have to attend classes. (He was studying some engineering course.) Then I walk in the street.'

ME: 'Do you always walk in the street when you have no classes?'

SASHA: 'No only when I have problems.'

ME: 'And you have problems now?'

SASHA: 'I need foreign money to buy a tape deck.'

ME: 'You do realize we have no foreign currency to change.'

SASHA: 'Yes, yes, I understand that; that is not why we are together.'

We walked away from the main street into side streets. All the buildings were very old and the pavements rough, the roads pot-holed and wet. The gutters held foul oily puddles. We looked down alleys, investigated yards discovered through once elegant arches. Typical was a place that looked as if it had been a mews — now the 'stables' were full of cranky old machinery not working and not manned. God knows what it was; Sasha didn't have a clue. Through one window I saw some women sewing on machines. The walls were peeling, the ancient stucco coming off revealing crumbling brickwork, the pediments from the doors were mostly gone as were the decorations round the windows. But there was enough left to see what a smart and posh place this had been — and even through the heaps of rubble and signs of poverty and squalor some Dickensian charm existed. I saw a strange bit of graffiti made with words written by it. I asked what did the words say. S: 'They are names — girls names — probably some children did it.'

It was getting on for lunch-time and citizens were forming queues at little food shops, buying soft drinks or sort of beer I think and eating what looked like little pies. I asked to see a bookshop and we were taken to one. It sold books from the GDR and all the wares were behind counters or in display cabinets. You could not browse. Harry bought some postcards and, when we left the shop, Sasha presented us each with a packet of postcards he had bought.

'A little gift,' he said. They were cards showing modern paintings in traditional style, and were awful; but it was impossible not to be touched by his present.

Harry argued with him as we walked on about our two systems of government. He entirely supported his own people and the Government. He admitted that there were weaknesses in the system and that in some ways the West was more advanced, but in spite of any inconvenience caused by the repressive and authoritarian regime he lived under, he believed in it. This was also true of Vera and Tatiana and of a beautiful young economics student we met on the train to Moscow a day later. It wasn't that they were not going to criticize the regime to a foreigner or that they were afraid to praise the West. You could say, I suppose, that they were thoroughly brainwashed; but it seemed to me more true to say they were fundamentally and completely foreign to us. They saw things differently, in ways I didn't understand, and they could not begin to imagine how we approached the same social problems and relationships.

It was even quite comic to think that we lived in a country ruled by the most incredibly benign ministers and officials compared to the Russians — yet we never stopped submitting our politicians, civil servants and trade union leaders to contemptuous and vehement criticism. They lived, by comparison, ruled by monsters, yet didn't speak badly of them. I was very well aware of the traditional fear of the police, the KGB and the recent terror of the Stalin purges — but, at that moment, that did not explain this phenomenon to me. It was exasperating. You felt Sasha should be raging about the rottenness of his city but he wasn't. We passed a hard currency shop. A glimpse through the door was enough to show the shelves packed with goodies — the whole atmosphere and look of the place stood out a mile.

HARRY: 'Doesn't it make people angry to see such places and to know they cannot enjoy these goods.'

SASHA: 'No — I don't think they particularly notice them.'

HARRY: 'Well now you've noticed it what do you feel?'

SASHA: 'Nothing. What should I feel? Envy? What good is envy? If I have enough to eat, somewhere to live and so on, why should I get het up about anyone else?'

Harry and I discussed this passive, fatalistic, apparently quite genuine reply. I said 'I feel he should be angry. Tell him in England if this state of affairs existed people would chuck rocks through the windows.'

Harry said: 'Do you think they would?' I said I didn't know.

Harry told Sasha that we must return to the hotel and asked him to accompany us as he'd like to give him a present. With no expression of gratitude or hesitation he simply fell in with this plan.

The sun was brightly shining on the canals and buildings. It had all the potential charm and beauty to rival Amsterdam, or possibly at its best Venice. Trying to find words to convey the atmosphere of these streets — once the Mayfair of chic Leningrad — I thought to myself it was like the far edges of a small provincial French town. You usually found yourself in such places when you were lost and you finished up nowhere, on the far side of the tracks on the edge of the industrial zone surrounded by pot holes, broken walls, gaping windows, and dirt. The big difference was that in France you could always find your way back — back to order and comfort, to wide roads, and shops in the town centre. Here the edge had come to the centre. There was no order. There was no way back — just the ludicrous exhortations: 'Citizens we must now, together, achieve the glorious aims of the eleventh five-year plan.' 'Citizens respect the work of the cleaners.' 'The highest aim of the Party is the good of the people.'

ME: 'What on earth would Lenin think if he could see this?'

HARRY: 'He'd think "great".'

ME: 'He couldn't.'

HARRY: 'This is what he wanted — a workers' state.'

ME: 'He could never have thought that in 1981 it would look like this.'

HARRY: 'I just don't know. He'd probably think "Bloody hell!" '

He told me a joke about Marx coming back to Russia and asking to speak to the people. He is told he can have an hour on TV, which is cut to half an hour, then to fifteen minutes, till eventually for complicated technical reasons he is given only five seconds. 'Citizens,' he says, 'I'm sorry!'

As we approached the hotel, Sasha turned off the Nevsky Prospect and pointed to a corner a block away. Harry explained.

'He doesn't want to come too near the hotel. It might not be wise. He'll wait for me there.'

'Is he afraid that after twenty-five years he may meet his first KGB man?' I said.

'Probably.'

We left him and walked on.

Near the hotel a man was unpacking one of a largish pile of cardboard boxes and instantly a queue began forming. Suddenly a gay and delightful atmosphere was created. People chatted and looked pleased and eager. The man and his assistant looked happy to be in the position to sell whatever it was they had. People were buying from him flat round tins about the size and shape of a small frying-pan, and with labels on the top.

Harry instantly joined the queue.

'What an incredible bit of luck,' he said. 'They are Russian herrings

— absolutely fabulous — one of the world's great delicacies. I must buy some.'

He asked a lady how many one was allowed. 'As many as you want,' she said, laughing at his greedy excitement. 'I'll buy six — no ten,' he said, planning already whom he would honour with such a priceless gift.

In the end he bought a whole carton-full. I think it was at least ten. It was heavy to carry. As we walked away a woman called something to him.

'Oh Christ!' he said, 'she says we must keep them in the fridge or they go off.'

'With a bang like an atom bomb I should think if all this goes up.'

'Bring the whole bloody hotel down.'

Laughing helplessly at our predicament we got to the hotel. One of us remembered the fridge in my room.

'Great, I'll put these in there.'

Off he went to deal with the fish and take Sasha his chocolate. I wanted to sit in the bar and write and wait for him.

After a bit he came back brimming over with pleasure.

'I'm in the herring business,' he said.

He had carted the fish upstairs and explained to the woman who gives you the keys to your room why he wanted to go to my room — and how he was worried about keeping so much fish until it could be consumed. She at once asked if she could buy some from him. 'Certainly,' he said. 'How many?' 'Six!' she said, 'OK.' He unpacked the carton, keeping four for himself. She gave him some money. 'No no! That's too much. They are 1 rouble 40 copecks, not 1.90', he said. She said that the price was 1.90. He pointed to the price on the tin — 1.40. 'It's wrong,' she said. 'It's what I paid,' he insisted. 'Nyet,' she was adamant, and for some reason wanted to pay more.

'What a weird country,' said Harry. (The fish stayed cool and safe in my fridge until we left.)

Harry had agreed to bring some presents to the mother of a Russian pianist who lived in Vienna. Earlier he had rung her and said we'd come that afternoon at 3.00. It was already time to leave so we got the stuff and set off up the still teeming Nevsky Prospect in a crowded bus to a tube also absolutely packed. Harry sat down and I remained standing. I looked at the row of men and women and tried to think what it was about him that would tell a Russian in an instant he was from the West. He was wearing no jacket, just a jersey, dark trousers and sort of casual running shoes. In the end it occurred to me that he simply looked more alert than the Russians slouching all around him. He was sitting up straight and his head was held high. From time to time he glanced around. Could that be it?

We emerged from the tube, remarking on the great speed of the very long escalators. At the point where they pitch you off there is a little inclined ramp to slow you down presumably. We found ourselves in a suburb. The open space outside the tube station was unpaved and muddy — it must be dreadful if it's raining, and the streets very wide. There were fewer people about but small groups were gathered near shops. In every direction columns of high-rise flats stretched into the distance. Not terribly high but the effect was to my eyes almost unbearably sad. What a hole to end up in. Funnily enough the ragged, weedy edges to the road made the place less horribly impersonal. The heaps of rubble and puddles and unfinished look of everything added a sort of human touch — you felt cats might hide and hunt there and children play, without boring institutionalized swings and adventure climbing-frames.

We found the tram and after a mile or so we got off it right opposite the old lady's block. We crossed the road, no doubt looking very conspicuous, and began searching for a door. We saw several but they appeared to be merely little tiny service doors, not the entrance to a large block of flats. Grass and weeds and shrubs, like a returning wilderness, grew right up to the rubble-strewn sides of the building. We picked our way towards one of the doors. Before we got to it it opened and there was a handsome, little old lady — actually pretty would be a better description. She had fine eyes and cheekbones, delicate features and a row of gold teeth. She was wearing slacks and a cardigan and had thrown a coat on to come downstairs to meet us. She was welcoming and shook hands firmly and she smiled all the time.

Inside this door there was a strong smell of paint and many signs of work in progress, for instance fresh unpainted plaster, new bits of wood, unprimed doors and so on. It was not grubby — more untidy, and it gave the impression of never having been finished rather than of decaying. The flats were ten years old.

We went up in a rickety little lift and entered her flat.

It consisted of a sitting-room, a bedroom, a kitchen and a bathroom and lavatory. It was not large but it was certainly not poky or small. I couldn't resist looking around and she beckoned me to go where I wanted. I looked into her bedroom. There was a sewing-machine on a table and on the floor rows and rows of onions — or perhaps bulbs of some other sort because there was no smell of onions.

The sewing-machine she explained was because, by the time she'd paid her rent, she would not have enough to live on unless she earned a bit extra. Her kitchen had a gas stove and a fridge. The door of the fridge was open for some reason—perhaps she was defrosting it. It was also empty, except for one or two bottles.

First of all Harry gave her the things her son had sent her. Shoes, tights, chocolate, olive oil, and so on — an odd higgledy-piggledy lot of stuff that she glanced at but expressed very little joy or pleasure at receiving. It was as if this was a pretty regular event. At least that was my impression.

Harry gave her a tin of herrings and asked her how to prepare them. She said it was complicated and you needed potatoes. Suddenly she said we could have some now and began peeling potatoes, preparing salad, cutting bread and so on.

All the time she talked about her younger son. About his childhood, his precocious talent for the piano, how he'd won a place at a musical academy at the age of five and graduated to be a very good pianist. But he would insist on doing things his way. He had fallen foul of the authorities and now had to live abroad.

I felt there was something very sad in this tale and her voluble telling of it. He was now her only son (her elder boy had been drowned five years ago), and she missed him dreadfully and told his tale to comfort herself. She was extremely volatile and lively, emphasizing her words with expressive gestures and smiling and laughing. Her voice was clear and powerful.

At last we sat down to eat. She showed us how to skin and bone the salted herring and she produced a bottle of good Austrian wine . . . 'because we are friends,' she said.

The fish was, as Harry predicted, delicious. We ate a lot but she barely tasted it — encouraging us to have more and filling our glasses. The fish was eaten with potatoes, salad and cheese. I took some cheese.

ME: 'It looks exactly like Cheddar.'

HARRY: 'What does it taste of?'

ME: 'Cheddar.'

HARRY: (to lady) 'Is this foreign cheese?'

LADY: 'No it's Russian.'

HARRY: 'What is it called?'

LADY: 'It's called Cheddar!'

HARRY: 'But that's English cheese.'

LADY: 'We'll I'm blowed!' (or words to that effect)

She had been in Leningrad all through the blockade and we began asking her about it. Never pausing to think for an answer, and speaking rapidly, she told us about it. For an hour or more the story poured from her — vivid memories of a terrible time — until she was almost in a trance and we listened spellbound. While she talked, often staring at me, Harry murmured a translation.

Her husband had been in the Red Army. He had joined up on the first day of the war. She was in Leningrad with two small children, a girl of six and a boy of eight or thereabouts. (The blockade lasted from September 1941 until January 1944.)

The city was not too greatly damaged; it was more like 'someone with several teeth knocked out'. She meant gaps in the buildings where shells and bombs had landed.

'People went mad with fear from the shelling. I told my children cowards die — the brave survive. When a shell landed next door I said "see we are not dead". I told them their Daddy would also survive because he is very brave. If you want to see a whole loaf of bread again, and your daddy again, then be brave.

'People starved to death in great numbers. On the worst day 19,000 died just from hunger, not counting the wounded soldiers. In the streets people queued for their rations and fell dead before they got their share. (Here she made falling gestures this way and that with her hands.) Policemen — officials — dragged the bodies away. I took my children's rations and cut them into little tiny portions. (She took a piece of bread and mimed dividing it up.) I fed it to them bit by bit through the day so their stomachs were never empty.'

'Did they complain of hunger?' I asked.

'No, they did everything I told them to. I made them take a little exercise each day even though they were so thin. Their skin was like stretched silk. (She pressed her fingers into her cheeks to show their drawn features.) I could count my ribs easily. In the morning I had to push my sunken eyes up again with my fingers before I could see. When I queued for rations I always took my children so that if we were shelled we would all die together.'

Eventually, when the blockade was lifted, she heard that her husband's unit, after suffering terrible casualties, had been withdrawn towards the East to rest and re-form. He asked her to come to him. There were lorries leaving across the frozen Neva. She was too weak to climb into the lorry and had to be helped. Her lorry was one of the last two of a convoy of six. Unknown to them the Germans had bombed the ice and the first four lorries carrying survivors sank into the freezing water. She did get out of Leningrad at last and made the fifteen-day journey to where her husband was. After six days together he left again for the front. She went from house to house asking for shelter for herself and her children. She found a woman who had several small children of her own who had to work all day in the fields. This woman had to leave her little ones alone all day so she took in the Leningrad refugee and her children, to help.

After some time she had to move on and went to relatives further west. Her little boy had to walk several miles to school. It had taken a year before the children began to look properly fed. When the blockade was lifted and food came in they were given soup. She swapped part of her ration for some sugar and chocolate. She was afraid of bloating her children with too much food and thought some sugar dissolving on their tongues would be better for them.

'People said I was crazy, but many died after the blockade from over-eating. The fifteen-day train journey also proved fatal to most of the passengers.'

By 1946 she was back in Leningrad and one day her husband returned.

'That must have been quite a meeting.'

'Yes — it was.'

'Did the children remember him.'

'Yes — but *they* had changed.'

'Do you find you think about these days now?'

'No — the death of my son has obliterated all that pain. When you lose a child it does not tear out half your heart — it tears out *all* your heart.' Even the death of her husband a year or so ago had not seemed anything like so terrible. He had been shattered by the death of his eldest son, and had never really recovered from it. She told us of a woman she knew who had lost seven sons in the war.

'Can you imagine . . .?' she paused.

'She has been left to grow old. She wanders like a dog without a home. If she hears the word "German" her grey hair stands on end.'

'Do you find you are upset by seeing German tourists perhaps?'

Very firmly she answered 'no'. She went on: 'Perhaps if I see one who is older, who is my age, I feel something — but the younger ones no. How could I? Some of them were born long after all this happened. It cannot be their fault — they cannot be blamed.'

All through this story she referred to the Germans not as 'Fascists' but using the phrase 'the Germans'.

When we first sat down to eat she had proposed a toast 'to peace — no more war'. It had smacked to me of a state ritualized toast. Now it seemed different. The toast made more sense. She had had enough. When she said 'no more war' she meant it — she really meant it. She said the older generation were afraid of war, but her grandchildren — they were not afraid of anything.

She showed us photographs of her children and husband and her wedding photograph. Her handsome young husband (a Jew whose family disowned him for marrying her) was seated and looking to the left. She appeared standing beside him, resting her head against his, ravishingly pretty, smiling and looking straight into the camera.

Now she proposed another toast:

'To the hope that this is not the last time we meet.' We drank.

It was time to go. She gave Harry some odds and ends to give to her son. Going down in the lift she prodded first Harry and then me in the chest. 'I would like to visit you, and I would like to visit you,' she said laughing.

'You would be very, very welcome.' She escorted us to a taxi rank and waited until one came. Then she shook hands and we left her.

The taxi bounced over the tram lines, swerved round a few pot holes and tore off towards Leningrad. She stood in her brown overcoat and raised a hand in farewell. To us she seemed lost in a ragged concrete jungle — out in the boondocks living in a '*1984*' nightmare among the proles. To her it just didn't seem like that. Her tragedies were there of course — the loss of her beloved older son and husband, the departure of the younger son abroad — but she had her daughter and other relations and friends. She was well fed and had work; she was well housed. Before she and her husband had got the flat they had lived in one room with two other families. But that was ten years ago and things were better now. She said that 'they' were forever putting pressure on her to move out of her flat. We thought at first she meant the housing authorities and felt angry on her behalf, but it turned out she meant her daughter and son-in-law — they wanted her to come and live with them.

In the evening I went to *Rigoletto* and Harry to the murder play he'd chosen.

The theatre was right round the corner from the hotel and pretty inside with tiers of boxes all round the auditorium. It was also almost full and as far as I could judge there were a fair number of tourists in the audience. A party of French men and women sat behind me and I get a great deal of pleasure from being able to understand snatches of conversation. You get so starved of making connections with people in a country where you cannot speak the language. In front of me was sitting a Japanese couple. The lady watched me drawing a box full of girls and a little boy.

When the overture began and the curtain went up the set was terrible — sort of Festival of Britain tat. In the centre of the stage was a tableau of Rigoletto looking a bit depressed and the shrouded body of Gilda. Somehow I couldn't get into the opera at all. I didn't like the singing, the acting, the costumes or the director's little touches. The music was OK but I yawned and yawned and knew half way through the first act I was not going to last the course.

I left in the interval — I felt exhausted and even wondered if I might be getting ill. I felt slightly sick and uncomfortable. I lay around in my room and wrote my journal.

Later Harry returned and we had a beer and some salad in a little restaurant.

Box at the Opera Leningrad

He had absolutely loved his play. A comedy about two men and a girl that sounded very good. He said the production bordered sometimes on the sentimental and there was a moment when, like the horrible little creature in a well known Chas Addams cartoon, while the rest of the audience were sniffling and crying he was stuffing a handkerchief into his mouth to suppress his laughter.

Saturday 10 October

This morning Harry wanted to sleep late so I got up, had breakfast and walked to the Hermitage. I made my way through different streets — wondering still at the unfinished street repairs everywhere, the piles of abandoned scaffolding, the dirt. It was odd dirt because there was no litter. Not even many cigarette ends. I emerged into the great open square or place by the Winter Palace and looked at the dome of St Isaac's above the trees to my left, and walked on to the entrance of the Hermitage. I was dismayed to find the pavement all round the entrance milling with people. On one side stood groups, Tartars, Germans, Finns, Russians, and on the other side a huge queue stretched away along the side of the Winter Palace.

I wondered what to do. I tried joining a group that was being let in but the Intourist guide was at the barrier checking her sheep in and it was impossible. I then noticed a sign which said that the museum opened at

47

Park in Leningrad

10.30 and it was still only about 10.00. I decided to go to look at St Isaac's and came back to try again later.

I walked through a little park and saw a statue of Gogol which pleased me and wandered round the closed Cathedral. I went back towards the river and watched some children and mothers, and one or two with their fathers, in a playground. I saw Catherine's statue of Peter The Great on his massive horse rearing up and gazing over the Neva.

Then I went back to the museum. The crown had vanished. The huge queue had simply gone in. Why they had come three-quarters of an hour early and patiently queued when it was quite unnecessary I just don't know. They were crazy.

I had a wonderful time in the nineteenth- and twentieth-century galleries. Particularly a Cézanne of a lady playing a piano, Morandi and Matisse. But it is a superb collection, and long before I was full I had to leave because we had been asked to vacate our rooms by 12.00 noon.

I hurried back to the hotel and in the Nevsky Prospect I saw the explanation of the Chekhovian scene of the horsemen I had noticed trotting past the hotel the day before. A film was being made, and a scene set in the days of the Revolution was being shot. What I had seen were extras going to the location. As I hurried on towards the hotel I had the most tantalizing and charming glimpse of old Leningrad.

Male and female film extras stood around waiting to go on. The men dressed in elegant top hats and overcoats with fur at the collar. The

Decembrists Square Leningrad

women in delightful Edwardian dress, muffs and little bonnets. There were carriages with top-hatted drivers wearing long overcoats with wide collars. The horses had old-fashioned harnesses and the street where they were became glamorous and lighthearted, charming and pretty. A whiff of comfortable middle-class life changed everything — and Leningrad could be seen as a great European city. If I was the authority here I would be careful about how many such films I should allow to be made in the streets of Russia. People might get the idea that there was something about the old days, difficult to define, which had a powerful attraction and an irresistible sweetness.

Back at the hotel I packed and left my things in Harry's room. Typically he had fixed it so that he didn't have to vacate it.

We had an hour or two to spare before our train left and thought we'd go to see the filming. I wanted Harry to get this tunnel view of the early 1900s in Leningrad. As we watched the film location and Harry took photos of the ancient cars and props, who should suddenly pop up again but Sasha.

Because we were in Russia, this most natural of meetings produced the thought: 'Is he following us?' Not that it would have made any difference even if he was. We shook hands and he joined us as he had before.

The sun was shining brightly and we walked by a canal, Harry having a circular political argument with Sasha about Poland. The Russian boy thought the Poles were hopeless and Solidarity a kind of western

Filming — Extras waiting on the Nevsky Prospect.

imperialist organization. His voice was never raised; he had none of the vivacity Russians are famous for.

Sometimes he smiled a little disbelieving smile.

We asked him to take us to pie shops for a snack. We ended up buying some little meat pies from a pie vendor on the pavement. They were deep fried in a sort of butter and a bit sickening. They cost 7 copecks each. Sasha refused one. He said they were made in a nearby factory.

Harry: 'Made in a factory — is it clean? So you don't have to worry about hygiene?'

Sasha: 'Yes you do have to worry about hygiene.'

I wanted some beer or tea and Sasha took us back to the film location and showed us a door — through curtained windows we could see people, mostly men drinking at tables.

We went in. It was the sort of place I would never go into unless I was taken — here in Russia I mean. There was no way of knowing whether you simply sat down or how you ordered what you wanted. The place had a dim interior and looked rather forbidding. The tall windows were all curtained. Some people were eating smoked fish, and sausage meat — most drank beer. At the door Sasha said 'Goodbye and Good luck'. We shook hands and he walked away — rather fast it seemed to me.

'Where's he off to,' I asked.

'Dunno — he didn't seem to want to come in. He asked me for my address.'

'Did you give it to him.'

'No — what's the point. Anyway I didn't trust him. What does he need my address for.'

'How did you refuse it. What did you say?'

'I said "perhaps it is better without addresses".'

50

The bar we were in was very tall, very long — like a great gallery — with many recesses going off to one side, each recess containing six tables with benches. On the pavement side the immense windows were curtained and the walls were uniformly a coarse-surfaced dull terracotta-to-blood red.

The waiters wore dinner jackets though the atmosphere was rough and somewhat grubby.

Harry soon discovered the form and we sat down at a table with two men, one in military uniform, and ordered smoked fish and beer. The fishes, like little smoked sprats, were OK. The beer was not. It was flat, cloudy, and left a sharp metallic taste in the mouth.

After a while we suddenly realized why the place had such a peculiar look to it. All the people sitting around were in costume. The soldiers were pre-revolutionary. A man near me was a coachman with a top hat. There were technicians as well, continuity girls and so on. But the strange dream-like atmosphere was largely caused by the period clothes and weapons that filled the place. Once you realized what was the cause the bar seemed less odd. The waiter explained that it had been taken over during filming for the film crew.

Naval Officer buying ice cream

Film extras in bar Leningrad

'Then why are we allowed here?' I asked Harry.

'We're foreign tourists — we can go anywhere!'

I think that is why Sasha sloped off so fast.

When the waiter noticed me sketching the interior he beckoned Harry away with him. After a while Harry came hurrying back. 'Leave all this,' he said, 'It's all upstairs — it's extraordinary.'

We climbed a little staircase and came out in a set of rooms as tiny, and intimate as downstairs had been huge and forbidding. Harry hurried me through two crowded rooms, ignoring someone who called out 'hey wait a moment', and we finished up in another little chamber. The first rooms had been dark and noisy, music was playing and there was a certain bustle. Here the room was empty and light and a young man with palette and brushes was engaged in covering the walls with pretty, bright murals.

He laid down his brushes and talked to us. He was slight and bearded, about twenty-five years old. He was completely relaxed and friendly and cool as a Frenchman. He didn't seem to be at all surprised at two Englishmen barging in. He explained he was decorating the room in an ancient Russian style with traditional scenes of medieval life.

Harry said: 'It's beautiful — like early church decorations.'

Artist: 'It's not like church decorations, there are no saints, except hidden ones.'

He smiled and pointed with his brush. Peeping through a window, watching a procession, his hands together as in prayer and round his head a golden halo, lurked a saint.

The painter's name was Danich and he showed us a strange self portrait he had done. In the background of a good competent likeness was a bloody red dragon — speared through and dying on a castle wall. He explained that the dragon was symbolic of the evil that was in Russia and in his picture it had been slain 'by an unknown force'.

He drew the dragon for me in my notebook — once again he showed it writhing in pain and holding a broken spear, on bloody claw aloft.

In return I drew a little caricature of him. He asked me to write my name and address on it. I looked inquiringly at Harry.

'Give it to him,' he said. 'He's OK.'

Danich said how long were we staying as he'd like to show us around — introduce us to some painters. 'We are leaving in an hour.' He shrugged and said 'pity'.

He was the most educated and the most western-like Russian we had met. A completely international type, and a charming young man.

I was already regretting having to leave Leningrad. The complicated reactions I had to the place were still very jumbled up but I was conscious of a strong feeling of affection and pleasure. I would have

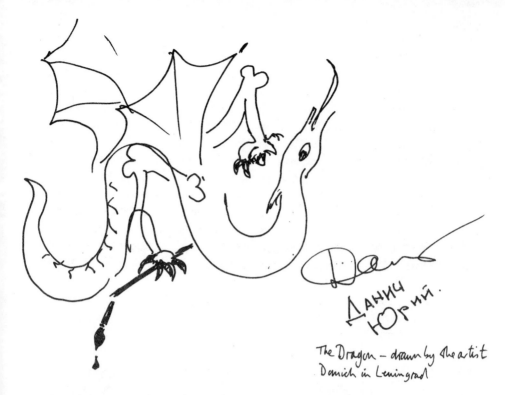

The Dragon — drawn by the artist
Danich in Leningrad

loved to meet the painter friends of Danich and to see a bit of his
Leningrad.

Back at the hotel we picked up our things from Harry's room. A
middle-aged cheerful looking old frump of a housemaid began talking
away to Harry.

'You are not leaving?'

'Yes we are off today.'

'You should stay longer — much longer.'

'We are going to Moscow.'

'Don't — no good can possibly come from it.'

Harry translated their little exchange: 'They don't like Moscow much
here, do they?'

The girl where we handed in our keys on the landing insisted on
getting a porter up to carry out bags.

One very old man in a cap arrived and picked up three heavy pieces of
luggage. I could hardly bear to see him staggering along with them and
tried to take one from him. He wouldn't let go. Downstairs an Intourist
car waited. No bills to pay, no hassle, into car, zoom off to station. No
need to pay car. Porter and Intourist girl waiting at station take us and
luggage to train.

'They really arrange things well don't they,' said Harry with great
satisfaction.

He was wearing tinted spectacles, a little pork pie hat, and a grey check overcoat. His trousers were well pressed and he had on shiny black shoes. I was wearing a Burberry raincoat and I had put on a tie. We looked very smart and unusual strolling down the platform behind the porter. My heart sank a little when I saw the train. It was very obviously 'hard class' as they call it. Nothing like the green monster that brought me here. This was a dirty old tramp of a train, and at the door of our wagon stood an old dragon taking tickets and generally organizing things. The Intourist girl pushed off.

As we arrived a load of coal was taken on board and put in a sort of little hopper just inside the door. I supposed it must be for some heating device, but it was not used during the journey as far as I could tell — and it was still there when we got out because I looked. It was impossible to find our places because so many of the numbers had fallen off the seats

View from J's hotel room

Attendant on train to Moscow

— so we just took two by a window. All the windows had curtains. When I tried to pull them back the whole lot, rod and all, fell down. In a strong Russian accent Harry said: 'This is considered by the authorities to be a clear case of sabotage.' I put everything back up.

The seats were a bit cramped — but not uncomfortable, and they had a reclining position if you preferred it. Nevertheless Harry went to see if it was possible to switch to a first class compartment. He came back soon saying there is no first class on this train. 'They are very surprised we are travelling "hard class". Foreigners don't.' I said: 'I'm afraid it's my fault, I asked to go by day because I wanted to see the countryside a bit. The first class is the night sleeper.'

'Never mind,' said Harry. 'It will be fun.' Strange and exotic looking people were getting on board; including a tartar in a padded overcoat, embroidered hat, and a red sash, a group of peasant women with handkerchiefs tied on their heads, some tough young workers and their girl-friends, as well as ordinary looking travellers. Sitting in the seat over the aisle from us was a startlingly pretty girl, very demure-looking in a high-necked blouse, and a fur-collared overcoat. She had a perfect complexion and extremely wide set large eyes.

The old conductress, her beret with it's great gold badge crossed hammer and spanner circled by a laurel wreath, huffed and puffed passengers into their places.

She looked a right old battleaxe. Needless to say within minutes of pulling out of the station Harry had charmed her completely. Her face wreathed in merry smiles she brought us beer, two kinds, and discussed which was superior. They tasted identical to me — and weren't bad. She showed us photographs of her lovely daughter and son-in-law and talked about preferring Leningrad to Moscow. When her duties compelled her to stay in Moscow—I think she lived in Vyborg—the railway authorities provided a special carriage for her and other workers to sleep in.

Soon we were slipping through the suburbs and out into the country. Here tantalizing views of little villages of wooden houses came into sight. Broken fences, carved window decorations, ragged gardens. In one village looking too like a Turgenev description for words I saw that the road between two rows of houses was merely rutted puddly grass, and an old man was leading two sheep across it. The desire to walk into such a village and get Harry to chat up a few peasants was very strong.

We settled down to the journey. Sometimes we talked over Leningrad, sometimes the old conductress ate Harry's salted almonds and bits of chocolate. Harry tried to persuade me to offer some to the pretty girl but I didn't have the nerve. I knew she would reply in Russian and I wouldn't know what she was talking about. Soon, of course, he swapped places with me so that he could offer her some chocolate which she very shyly took. She was slower than some to fall under his spell but she talked. She was an economics student and they began a discussion about the Russian and western economies. I probably wouldn't have understood too much even if the conversation was in English, but from time to time Harry translated. She was a very bright girl indeed and several times her replies to Harry's somewhat challenging remarks were neatly fielded and thrown back, and he would add to the translation: 'Clever girl this.' She was gradually getting more chatty and interested. She had an engaging trick of snapping her fingers to emphasize a point. Harry suddenly looked up and half rose to his feet. At the other end of the carriage a great disturbance was going on.

'There's a fight,' he said.

There is a particular look to a fight. It is often made up of flurries of violent movement followed by moments of stillness which then give way to wild punching and grappling. It was impossible to see what was happening but at least five or six men seemed to be involved and several girls looked on.

The old conductress marched down the aisle remonstrating, and all eyes stared at the struggling group. Her intervention was completely ineffectual and she left the carriage looking very angry. The struggle reached a climax of swinging fists and lunging bodies and more or less all the combatants disappeared from view below some seats. Great cries and groans could be heard and vicious battering noises. 'They are giving someone quite a going over,' said Harry.

The conductress reappeared with a guard and they both approached the fight, stayed a while, and then left again.

For the next hour or so all was quiet, except every now and then a bloodcurdling moan could be heard as if some creature was in great distress. One was.

What had happened was that a drunk had annoyed a girl who had left the carriage to go to the lavatory. When she returned he followed her and was promptly jumped on by her friends. They were now sitting on him until the train reached the next station.

The pretty girl was horribly embarrassed by this scene and wanted us to know that it was not something that happened every day. We must not form any sort of judgement on this one unfortunate and disagreeable incident.

'It will be interesting to see what happens,' said Harry to me. 'I imagine we will be invaded by an army of police as soon as we stop.'

At last the train pulled into a station and to our surprise for a long while, or what seemed quite a long while, nothing happened. Then a small policeman in a greatcoat and cap walked in. 'Here we go,' said Harry. The policeman took a look, spoke a few words and left again. A moment later he arrived back with one of the most frightening looking men I've ever seen.

He was not tall but roughly square. He had a black narrow brimmed hat on the back of his block-shaped neckless head and he had on a black jacket of slightly shiny looking mock leather. His face was expressionless, and strangely blank.

When these two got to the drunk they at first appeared to be handcuffing him but actually they were unbinding his wrists which had been tightly secured with a belt. Then, one going before and one behind, they led an incredibly rough and considerably battered-looking man by the hands, down the carriage towards us. The man looked vaguely around, angry and bewildered, blood trickled from his nose. His tangled hair stood up all over his head. Just before they reached us, he made a struggling movement as if to say 'let go'. The two men had been leading him almost gently — as an injured child might be led — but the instant he made as if to free himself the policeman and his colleague acted with savage speed. With skilful and sudden twisting movements the drunk's arms were wrenched up behind his back and locked there, two hands reached for his head, grabbed handfuls of hair, and he was hauled backwards. The man was helpless and obviously in terrible pain.

Policeman and druzhénnik arresting drunk on train to Moscow

Even at that moment, ugly though the scene was, part of me was very relieved that the policeman and his companion were there and were so devastatingly efficient. Nasty though they were, they were also on my side as it were, and the bleary, bloody, mindless drunk was slightly nastier.

As they got to the narrow end of the carriage the poor man made another futile struggling movement. It was hard to see whether or not it was deliberate, but with a bang his head was crashed against the wall leaving a bloody smear and the last I saw of him was his bent back and upraised face as they frog-marched him away down the platform into the night.

We asked the girl and the conductress what would happen to the man. They said his punishment could be severe. His head might be shaved and he would go for fifteen days detention or hard labour. His employers would be informed and he would lose any privileges he might have earned at his place of work. He could be fined, have to take his summer holiday in the winter and if he was on a waiting list for a car or apartment he'd be put back down the list a certain amount. The two women talked a bit about alcoholism and discussed the problem.

Later the old conductress said she would love to travel. She'd love to go to France and Italy and see the Italian national costumes. 'When you travel abroad you recover your elan, your spirits are revived.'

The journey didn't really seem all that long and by 10.30 p.m. or so we were entering Moscow. Even from the train it looked different from Leningrad. It looked huge and more modern. Less tatty. Perhaps I was already just beginning to get used to being in Russia — perhaps because I was with Harry and I knew he would fix everything that might crop up, but I wasn't so excited getting off the train here as I was in Leningrad.

It seemed much more like a bloody great modern city. It may sound a bit unlikely but I was reminded of London. There was none of the glamour of decayed eighteenth- and nineteenth-century splendour that was such a striking feature of Leningrad. Smoothly Intourist swept us up, popped us into a taxi and we sped off into Moscow.

My first impression stayed with me until we passed Red Square and I saw the great walls of the Kremlin. That gave me a jolt. All the bogeymen side of this vast, terrifying country became very real. I felt a tingle of fear.

When we stopped at the hotel I suddenly longed for Leningrad. This wasn't the same. It was an old hotel and it turned out a comfortable and pleasant enough one but it didn't have the eccentric dotty charm of the Leningrad hotel.

We checked in and were told that although the restaurant was now closed we could eat there — the restaurant would be informed. Our luggage was taken to our rooms and we went straight to eat.

It was astonishing. The restaurant was very big and had a fountain playing in the middle. All round the walls enormous mirrors reflected plants and pillars, gilt and stained glass decoration.

Round the fountain were dancers, several had given up moving and clung together, kissing. One man held his partner in a curious way, his hands resting lightly on her breasts. I was almost shocked — nay I *was* shocked. This was very improper. There were tables full of girls, Arabs,

Russians — all apparently fairly drunk, everywhere you looked. I saw a man throw a glass of champagne over the legs and feet of some friends leaving his table — they skipped and laughed and staggered away.

The atmosphere of the place was wicked, naughty, racy — very unlike the boisterous but friendly restaurants we'd been in in Leningrad.

Moscow Restaurant

We ordered the usual. Vodka, caviare and smoked salmon, and added lemonade. While we waited for it the band packed up and the crowd melted away. Even before the food came the lights began to go out and the great glass gilt and marble interior became gloomy and shadowy.

'This is too much,' said Harry. He got up and, shoulders back, head slightly on one side, he marched confidently and angrily across the deserted dance floor to an alcove where a cluster of waiters stood. He disappeared and within seconds all the lights came on again and he reappeared grinning broadly.

'You are amazing,' I said.

'They are not used to people complaining,' he said. 'It throws them completely.' He explained that he did it for their own sakes as much as for his own. 'So they will know what sort of standards western visitors require. . . . Otherwise how will they know?'

The food was delicious and an hour later we turned in.

Sunday 11 October

As we left the Hotel Metropole we could see spires from the Kremlin sticking up into the sky beyond the buildings to the left. We had nothing particular to do. Nigel Wade, the *Telegraph* man in Moscow, had invited us to dinner and was picking us up at 7.00 p.m. The day was empty so we headed for the spires.

The Kremlin was smaller than I expected and much more beautiful. Behind the curtain walls attractive yellow buildings and graceful onion domes of gold soared into the sky like tethered hot-air balloons. The presence of St Basil's Cathedral at the far end of the square, with its beautifully striped, cut-patterned domes, lightened whatever grimness there was in the high walls and guarded entrances of the Kremlin. Only the Lenin mausoleum ruined the sweep and romance the place might have had. It squatted, hideous and immovable, sucking an endless river of people through itself — the queue moved very slowly, shuffling patiently forward to see 'the doll' as one Muscovite put it to us.

It was very hard to understand the size and patience of this queue. It stretched for hundreds of yards, winding across the square down a slope round a corner into a park where it turned and ran on and on into the trees — orderly, slow, boring and horrible. What on earth did they think they were doing? To wait for hours and hours and hours — to see what? It was the most mysterious sight — perhaps they believed in magic, a kind of red ju ju?

We tried in a half-hearted way to jump the queue — foreign tourists could — but even Harry failed to fix this, and I didn't care. My western attitudes were too strong to take this deifying of a man. I found it disgusting. I wanted to deluge the streets with badges reading: 'Honk your horn if you haven't seen Lenin.' Or: 'I went to Moscow and didn't visit the mausoleum.' Someone told us a day or two later that the Soviet system would last so long as people were prepared to queue in this way for this object.

We wandered about, looking at St Basil's Cathedral and the thousands of tourists taking photographs and chattering. Then we left the square heading across the river towards the Tretyakov museum. The Moscow skyline was made ugly enough by dull modern buildings but Stalin-style skyscrapers, all concrete and spikes, made it vaguely menacing as well. They looked like broken teeth or claws scratching at the sky.

Once over the bridge, leaving the Kremlin on our left, we found ourselves in a very different kind of street. There were low terraces and individual houses, with little gardens. The usual litterless dirt and rubble, but not without charm.

We looked at a deserted church where a man with two big white dogs told us that this place was being renovated but there was another 'working' church nearby. As we left him his dogs barked and snapped at our heels. I swung my bag at one and it bared its teeth. Harry made a threatening gesture and the stupid nasty animal cringed.

'See — bloody coward,' said Harry. Walking on in the direction of the other church we saw huge queues outside the Tretyakov museum. People were being let in in squads of about twenty. We decided to go on. A woman seeing us hesitate told us to come back on Tuesday, when the museum would be open and much emptier.

Soon we found ourselves in a little tiny park or open space. The ground under the trees was only hard earth but there were seats and little fences and bits of garden. Across the other side of this spot we could see a large church. Its walls were pale yellow and its lovely domes were golden and they shone softly through the autumn leaves. A few people sat in the garden; others moved towards the church.

We walked up to the church, stepped inside and felt every sense soothed as the door silently swung shut behind us. The dim interior was lit by candles whose reflected lights flickered from gilt, glass, gold and silver decorations. The church was sweetened by incense and beautiful singing filled the air, a chant that rose and fell like wind through trees, dying and falling — almost ending — and rising again. Lovely colours drenched the whole scene — sunlight fell through high windows on to murals and paintings and at the far end of the church was a magnificent altar blazing and glittering with light, mysterious and magnetic. The entire congregation stared forward, singing, and each individual from time to time crossed himself or herself earnestly. The old women made lovely wide gestures, their arms moving slowly and gracefully across their bodies, and as they completed the movement their arms dropped to their sides and they bowed.

We stepped forward towards the altar and stood watching priests going through a complicated service, appearing and disappearing, sometimes carrying holy objects. They were all, even the youngest and

64

most lowly, wearing embroidered robes. One wore a full black head-dress, one had high cheekbones, staring deep-set eyes and a wispy beard, another a clean-shaven face with long curly hair that fell to his shoulders.

For a moment, there was silence then a man's voice spoke some words and the congregation replied; from behind a screen a chorus began to sing. It was the most moving and beautiful music I've ever heard.

'What is it?' I whispered to Harry.

'I don't know. It's wonderful isn't it?'

'Mmm.'

'Is it a recording — I've never heard such singing.'

'No — look you can just see them singing through there.'

'They must be professionals.'

While the choir sang the people continued to cross themselves from time to time. There were many old, old women in the church but there were also young people and even a number of children. The devout fervour with which they all attended to the service was unmistakable. The ardour with which they stared at the altar was so passionate and intense, and illuminated by the candles, the filtering sunshine and the thousands of twinkling points of reflected coloured lights, the sight was unforgettable.

'The Communists can never match this,' murmured Harry. 'Never in a million years.'

'It's like being given a drink when you are thirsty,' I said. I was trying to express the effect of coming unexpectedly on this extraordinary scene right in the heart of Moscow. Moscow, dominated by the Kremlin, with its awful, depressing mausoleum; the mindless queueing to see the 'doll'. The scores of police everywhere, the dreadful Lubianka building and the odour of fear and uncertainty that pervades Russian life — and here, like a refreshing drink, there was music and gentleness and passion and certainty, and great beauty.

The service continued with a procession through the church led by an old Archimandrite, looking like Matisse, with spectacles, a white beard, and magnificent garments. Old ladies got to their knees as he passed by, some bent down to touch the ground. He returned to the altar and spoke. After a while Harry said: 'He's telling the parable of the fishermen, you know the one where he says "follow me and I will make you fishers of men".'

'Sounds a dodgy sort of sermon for here doesn't it?'

'Mmm — can't really mistake his message can you?'

Now and then while he spoke someone would press forward to kiss his hand or perhaps the silver cross he wore round his neck. Once he murmured something to a young woman who had come forward and hesitated. He held the cross towards her.

'He's telling her not to be afraid,' whispered Harry. She kissed the cross and hurried away into the crowd.

When he finished and after he had given his blessing we walked out with the crowd, and back across the bridge and over Red Square.

At the hotel we asked the waitress who served us lunch (a cheerful black-haired maiden with the most lovely complexion) whether she knew the church we'd been in.

'No,' she said, 'But the Bishop of all Moscow has lunch here almost every day.' Later when Harry returned from going to the loo he said: 'I've just seen the Bishop. He's having lunch next door, (We were in the cafe, he was in the restaurant) chatting to the waiter. Guess who he is.'

66

'The Archimandrite from the church?'

'Yes.'

Harry began writing the old man a note. The gist of it was that we were two visiting Englishmen who had come to his church and attended his sermon and been so mightily impressed that we would be grateful for the chance to speak to him and pay our respects.

When he'd finished he asked the girl to take it to the Bishop. She looked embarrassed and said she was not allowed into the restaurant. Could she take it and give it to one of the waiters to deliver? She'd rather not. Harry decided to take it himself but when he got to the restaurant the priest had gone and although we looked for him several times we never saw him again.

The hotel was comfortable and the service quite good. It was difficult for me to tell much because Harry did all the ordering and had this knack of charming and engaging the interest of the waiters and waitresses. But on the few times I ate alone — at breakfast for instance — they were perfectly OK. You did feel in your Intourist hotel with it's hard currency shops and bars that you were very well insulated from the harsh life the Russians were living all round you. And the surroundings had a great deal of charm — in the hotel I mean. The pillars and marble and mirrors and chandeliers were all, in their faded way, beautiful. In the long and winding passage that led from the lift to my room a small squad of Bill Tidy-like women were repairing the cracked and flaking plaster on the walls. They were wearing dungarees and handkerchiefs round their heads and they worked slowly and badly. Even where they had finished, the walls and doors still looked incomplete and messy. If you nodded or smiled at them to indicate some sort of apology for disturbing their work as you passed they regarded you with an utterly blank Russian stare that was either a sign of profound hostility or impenetrable stupidity. Hard to tell which — perhaps it was a Russian thing I didn't understand. During the days I was here this shoddy work continued at a very slow pace.

I spent the afternoon of this day writing in my room.

In the evening Nigel Wade picked us up in his car and took us to his flat for dinner — an excellent Chinese meal he and his wife Chris cooked. His flat, with office attached, was splendid and roomy.

There was much conversation about how much we were being watched and bugged. As far as I could gather you assumed everywhere was bugged and everyone could be going to report you to 'the organization', the KGB. So you got careful — used public telephones, dropped your voice, did not mention places or names. It was like an endless children's game that had rapidly become tiresome and had a menacing reality at the centre of it. The telephone in Nigel's flat had a neatly printed sign on it: 'This telephone is not secure.'

Nigel offered to take us to a village 20 kilometres or so outside Moscow the following afternoon — so that we could see some countryside and visit Pasternak's grave. We leapt at the chance.

One little incident occurred that evening. Harry had met two actresses in Leningrad who were having breakfast at our table one morning. When they heard he was coming to Moscow one of them gave him a phone number to ring so that she could organize some tickets to a play she was appearing in at the Satire Theatre. She gave the phone number of her friend because she said: 'My husband has a certain position'. I think he was in the navy, but anyway it might have been awkward for him to be telephoned by an Englishman. I must emphasize that her discretion about her own phone number was nothing to do with any improper developments this friendship might produce. Her secretiveness was simply caused by the system.

When we first got to Moscow Harry had called the girl whose number he had been given and she had said: 'Wonderful! you are here! Good! welcome! Ring me back on Sunday evening and we'll fix up to give you the tickets. Have a good time meanwhile.'

Harry asked Nigel whether he could phone the girl — and would it be wise to go out and find a telephone. In the end he did go out to a nearby phone box — but the police guard could easily have seen where he was going and if ever a phone should be tapped, that one, right by the foreigners compound, would be an obvious choice.

After a bit Harry came back — smiling and looking conspiratorial. 'Did you get through?', we asked. 'Yes,' he said, 'I got through all right. Someone else answered the phone and told me my friend was not there. She left Moscow unexpectedly.'

This mystery was left unsolved. Was she there but had second thoughts about this contact? Had she been warned to stay away from foreigners perhaps by her friend's husband? Had the KGB listened to the original phone conversation and scared her away? Or was her departure for some professional or personal reason that was quite innocent? We never found out — but it seemed unlikely that if the last was true she would not have left a message of some sort for Harry.

One way or another, perhaps because Harry made so many contacts with Russians, we nudged up against this dark and threatening side of Russian life constantly.

When Nigel drove us home he took us via the British Embassy where he had to collect something. It was about midnight and the streets were almost deserted. He pulled up outside the guarded Embassy gates and said: 'I'll just pop in; I'd say come too but you'd never get in without a pass.' We saw him go up to the guard and show a pass and he walked up the drive towards the superb eighteenth– or early nineteenth-century mansion that is now our Embassy.

Harry and I got out to look at the breathtaking view. Directly across the river on whose bank we now stood was the Kremlin. The great golden domes spotlit and glowing, the brilliant red stars on its great spires hanging in the dark sky, and its walls bleak and magnificent.

The police guard we noticed was opening two great metal gates that led to the Embassy drive. He bowed, saluted and beckoned us to enter, grinning cheerfully as if to say 'come in — come in, don't hang about out there'. So in we went. 'Never get in without a pass', we said to each other simultaneously. Nigel seemed surprised to see us and we asked the man on the door could we just look inside. 'Of course,' he said in a friendly way. Nigel introduced us to him and the duty officer at the desk — we chatted for a while. It amused me to find this little patch of England here in this most strange and foreign country.

Monday 12 October

I was beginning to worry quite a bit about my Polish visa. If it came I could get on my train to Warsaw and everything would be OK. If it didn't come, my Russian visa would run out and I would have no way booked for getting out of this place. I planned if possible to fly to Vienna and stay with Harry for a couple of days if the visa didn't get through. Harry had been assured it had been granted and would be sent to the Moscow Polish Embassy.

We went early in the morning to the Embassy but they'd never heard of my application; no message had come through. One felt helpless. No there was nothing they could do, no they could not issue a transit visa without confirmation from Warsaw — sorry they would do what they could and would we return on Wednesday morning. But we explained that if on Wednesday morning he said 'no', that didn't give me much time to make other arrangements. Shrug. Tough titties.

We left — my anxiety somewhat increased. Harry was still optimistic however. He said we'd telex his Polish friend in Warsaw. A big shot who could fix it if anyone could and who had already assured Harry that my visa was granted.

Harry had also resourcefully rang another contact he had, 'the sister of a friend' who it turned out, surprise, surprise, was an actress and was also appearing in the same play: Mayakovski's *The Bed Bug* at the Satire Theatre. She had fixed two tickets for that evening and had invited us to her flat for something to eat afterwards. Harry certainly falls on his feet. He was now dying to see whether his other friend would appear on stage that night — thus destroying the story that she had left Moscow.

On our way back to the hotel for lunch (we went there in the hope of seeing the Archimandrite) we stopped off at GUM — the huge store occupying the whole of one side of Red Square — to see it and to buy some notebooks. We did see it and found the building absolutely terrific, but the crowd quite impossible and the goods lousy. I bought some lined notebooks which were not what I wanted and we left. Later a Russian laughed when he heard we'd been there. 'We would never shop there,' he said, 'it's impossible.' He told me where to go to find the sort of notebooks I wanted — but in fact I never got round to it.

In the afternoon we took a taxi to Nigel's flat. We passed the horrible, obscure, Lubianka building with its statue to some grisly mass-murderer outside it. As we went by Harry wound down the window and took a couple of pictures of it. The driver noticed what he was doing and the following conversation occurred.

TAXI DRIVER: 'They won't come and take us away will they?'

HARRY: 'Surely not.'

TAXI DRIVER: 'If you ever go in there you won't come out alive' (chuckling).

HARRY: 'But that was all in the past wasn't it?'

TAXI DRIVER: 'Yes yes — that's true — now it is merely an historical monument.' He was serious by now and added a little later: 'But they might get a little jumpy if you start to take photographs from a car.'

HARRY: (to me in English) 'That's probably the understatement of all time.'

At that moment a police car pulled up alongside us, the officers inside all looking straight ahead, but I felt a twinge of fear, a paranoid thought: 'Christ! they got on to us quickly. . . .'

At Nigel's flat Harry telexed Warsaw and I sent a telex message to Caroline. Nigel showed us newish *Daily Telegraphs* and I read more about Sadat and the SDP and a Tory row involving Heath criticizing Tory policy. . . . It all seemed far away and, except for sending a message to Caroline, rather unreal.

We drove with Nigel — he had a driver but said he couldn't find him! — out through Moscow. It was really like driving through any big European town. Bloody great boring building — high-rise blocks and urban throughways. Only the Stalinist skyscrapers, the Communist party slogans, and the occasional gigantic portrait of Lenin kept you reminded of where you were — and perhaps the lack of colour that advertising brings to western cities. The unrelieved drabness was an important part of Moscow's views, unrelieved that is except for the churches. Like the Leningrad painter's hidden saints the domes of Moscow's churches were there, half hidden, but pretty and charming and putting so much of the rest to shame.

As we got out into the country life looked less grim — as I suppose is always the case to some extent, when you leave a city. Outside in the country little wooden houses backed on to fields, beech and pine forests stretched away on all sides. We stopped and walked through a damp autumny wood to a recreation area. We came to a lake with summer-houses and changing sheds, now deserted but for one middle-aged couple who sat on a bench at the peaceful scene. In the summer this is a popular swimming place and in the winter Muscovites ski through the surrounding woods.

Sometimes behind fences and mostly hidden from sight we could glimpse the dachas of some privileged big wig or Party member. We drove on to the village of Peredelkmo, where I drew the picturesque houses and Nigel and Harry took photographs of the lake and the bridge. It was very pretty and felt quite calm and tranquil — miles from the ugly side of Moscow. It was true that monster airliners screamed and roared overhead quite frequently, coming in to land at a nearby airfield but they tend to do that in England too. . . . The best part of our little tour was visiting Pasternak's grave. It lay under some trees near the top of a slight rise, and his grave and the area round it was bright with vases and jam jars full of flowers. Into the gravestone which bore a portrait in relief of the great writer someone had crudely scratched the lopsided cross of the Russian Orthodox Church. It did not seem to me vandalism — like the flowers, it was a human touch.

Pasternak's grave outside Moscow

We walked back through the graveyard chatting about my notebooks. Nigel considered it dangerous to try to take them through the Russians' customs check on the train. It's the sort of thing they don't like. He even offered to try to get some diplomat to carry them home or he would bring

village outside Moscow

them when he was due to fly out in six months time. Or he would photograph them so that at least there was a record of them should they get confiscated. My feelings swung wildly. He could be right, in which case I was very depressed, or it could be unnecessarily alarmist. Harry was undecided.

By the graveyard was a church and we walked up to it. From the outside it looked deserted. Inside you stepped at once back into a magic world. The same dim light as in the other church that sparkled with candles and coloured reflections — bold murals and pillars, shadows and the smell of incense. A group of old ladies were chanting some part of a religious service — one leading and several others responding. Still others stood apparently praying, crossing themselves and bowing.

I have sometimes been in churches where I have felt oppressed by the wealth and self satisfaction of the place, irritated by the mumbo jumbo and feeling that it's a kind of a trick — the promise of some future, distant, holy reward that does not in any way help the urgent material needs of the devout who prayed so hard for so much. Here I felt no such feelings. I felt there was something splendid and hopeful in the very existence of such a refuge from the everyday world. Here was some spiritual nourishment that a country and a system spectacularly failed to provide in any other way and which in some form or other was needed.

We drove back into Moscow down the highway. Every now and then you saw a Chaika, the big black cars used by privileged Russians, and more rarely an enormous curtained Zill, black shiny and ugly. Otherwise the cars looked small and tatty. There were many big lorries and police jeeps (or maybe they were military, I forgot to ask).

Outside the Metropole we said goodbye to Nigel and prepared to go to the theatre. Harry carried a little bag of presents — chocolate, coffee, etc., for Vera, the sister of his friend. She had agreed to meet us outside the theatre to hand over the tickets.

Harry, who stands out a mile in London with his tweed hat and old pale check overcoat, was unnecessarily anxious about whether she'd find us. I said I thought she'd find us. I said I thought she'd pick us out — even though the foyer of the theatre and the pavement outside was packed with jostling Muscovites. Sure enough she did. A very attractive snub-nosed girl with long hair and big smile approached us and handed us tickets and said to me in halting but good English: 'I think you will understand every word.' She then told Harry the story line in Russian which he translated for me. She gave us another lovely smile and vanished saying she'd meet us again here after the play.

When he was leaving his coat Harry somehow jumped the queue. The women spoke to him. 'I'm English tonight,' he said to me. 'I can't understand a word she's saying.' The woman, realizing it would be

74

Peredelkino

quicker to simply take his coat to get rid of him, did so, and Harry walked away satisfied.

The audience was distinctly middle-class. Well-dressed women and men in suits and ties — not all, but enough to give a smart look to the theatre. It could have been an audience in London except for the uniforms of the military men who were quite numerous. Harry's acquaintance from Leningrad did not appear; her part was taken by another actress. The play was done with considerable vigour but little imagination. I was not bored by it but understood rather little although Vera's account plus Harry's whispered translations got me through it quite well. As we were leaving the auditorium to get coats at the end of the play we were stopped at the exit by a lady — obviously because there was such a crush at the cloakroom place that more people barging in

75

would only slow things up. It was a sensible yet irritating incident and we wondered whether Londoners would put up with it. Probably not we thought.

As we were leaving the theatre a boy approached me in the crowd and said 'Are you English?' He spoke slowly with a very strong accent and was about seventeen or eighteen years old.

'Yes,' I said.

'I collect your money,' he said.

'I have no money to change,' I said, amused by his quaint English. He smiled and insisted: 'Yes, it is good for me.'

'Mm — but I haven't got any.'

'Not got any?'

'No — sorry.'

He moved away but at the exit he came up to me again.

'Long live the friendship between our two great countries.'

'I'll shake on that,' I said shaking his hand. 'Yes,' he said. I couldn't make this last little exchange out. The next day when I mentioned this incident to Anton (a Russian friend of Harry's) he said:

'It was a joke — he was joking.'

'He didn't seem to be.'

'It was a joke.'

Harry suggested it was a phrase he had learnt at school and was merely saying it because he could say it. I thought it was like a reflex — he had been told so often about his country and Government fighting for peace, and indivisible bands being forged by the struggle, that the thought and words popped out parrot-like. Anton could not believe it: 'It was a joke,' he said. 'No one could be so bloody silly,' he seemed to be saying, 'to mouth such a pat phrase without intending to be funny.'

Outside we met Vera and congratulated her and told her how good the play was, as one does, and she said: 'Thank you, now let us go home and have something to eat.' We walked towards a bus stop I could see a hundred yards away but half-way there she stopped and, raising her arm, began to flag down passing cars. A few sped past but one or two stopped but drove on after a quick conversation. Then another stopped after she had stepped dangerously far out into the road waving vigorously. 'OK,' she said, and we all got in.

The system is just that instead of taking a taxi you take anyone who'll take you. The price is fixed 1 rouble, 2 roubles, 3 roubles before the journey and it's done on a distance basis, so much a kilometre. Our journey was going to cost 1 rouble. The first three cars had driven on because they only wanted to take someone who was going on a three- or four-rouble ride. One was not worth their while.

I asked if we were taking our driver out of his way. 'Was he going here anyway?'

Vera stopping cars in Moscow

'I don't know,' she replied 'Maybe, maybe not.'

She said she would not get into just anyone's car if she was alone — and not after dark at all probably unless she was desperate — but this system was widely used, and it was extremely rare to hear of citizens coming to harm by using it. After we were told about it we frequently saw people flagging down cars although it was illegal private enterprise. We stopped and paid and got out in a street of the usual white-coloured highish-rise flats and walked over to one and rode up in a lift quite high. Out into the hall, all this clean but impersonal, and through her front door which was opened by Mischa, Vera's boy-friend with whom she lived. He was short, handsome, with thick dark hair and a beard. He spoke excellent English and had a somewhat reserved and withdrawn manner. She was talkative and flighty — a bit of a show-off — he was intelligent, sober and cool. The flat was comfortable and warm. Wall-to-wall carpeting, plenty of books, not too brightly lit. There were almost no pictures anywhere — something that always bothers me in a house — the walls were bare, but once more we could have been almost anywhere in the world.

Vera had prepared a chicken with apples and it was very good indeed. There were grapes and, to drink, a very strong home-made spirit the colour of Ribena.

The conversation ranged widely over many subjects but always returned to a sort of running comparison between the East and West. Each time a subject was laid aside one felt all one had achieved was some sort of illumination of the basic, simple, truth that we were very, very different from one another.

Although Mischa felt it was necessary to learn from the West as much as possible, although he felt in some ways we were ahead of the Soviet Union, he never uttered a word of reproach against the lunatics who ran his country and clearly associated himself totally with his country, his Government and his fellow citizens. Like the ape man who helped the policeman take away the drunk on the train, Mischa was a 'druzhinnik', a volunteer policeman who once or twice a month went out on patrol to help keep the peace. ('As if there aren't enough bloody police in this place already', said Harry later.)

'Recently, a few years ago, there was a problem with hooliganism here in Moscow, but the police and the Party have dealt with it. We don't get much now.'

'How did they deal with it?'

'They caught some hooligans and the punishment was severe.'

'How severe?'

'Oh maybe five years hard labour and loss of certain privileges, fines and so on.'

We didn't ask him to describe hard labour here but I don't imagine it's a hell of a lot of fun.

I asked him what he actually did if he saw some young men who, in his opinion, were behaving badly.

'I go to them and say "don't do that".'

'What if they carry on?'

'Well they probably won't carry on. You see I have a card. They are very afraid of that.' He showed us his neat shiny card with its hammer and sickle on the front.

'If they are uncooperative I go somewhere and call the police.'

'And they come quickly?'

'Yes very quickly.'

'What if the hooligans attack you?' This question seemed to puzzle him a bit.

'Attacking me would be the same as attacking a policeman — the punishment would be the same.'

The implication was you'd have to be absolutely barking to even think of doing anything so rash.

'The punishment would be severe.'

'Yes.'

Vera told us that she had twice been called to 'that place'. She made a shushing gesture, shook her hands and said quietly smiling mischievously: 'We don't mention its name.' She meant the Lubianka.

'What happened?'

'I got a phone call telling me to go for a talk.'

'Who from?'

'I don't know.'

'What did you do?'

'I went of course.'

Both times it had been because of contacts she had had with western men. One had been a diplomat from the USA I think. Both times the first question had been the same.

'Why did you tell your friend(s) that we wanted to see you?'

'Were you afraid?'

'Yes of course.' But she went on to explain that in a way she was a marked woman because her sister had married a foreigner and now lived abroad. This was enough to make her fall under suspicion so she thought that she had little to lose.

Mischa smiled and said: 'Vera is a radical . . . And she is a savage to serve us food but no napkins.' He grinned and held up his hands, greasy from the chicken bones. We laughed and Vera ran out to get paper napkins. It was difficult to return to the fascinating subject. Somehow Mischa, one felt, disapproved.

Vera began to talk about some folk music she had heard and learnt about. Recently it has become more popular and fashionable. She told us the story of one ancient song. It concerned a young woman who was going away to be married. Her parents begged her not to go. Some swans flying about came into it and some girl-friends who also expressed the desire to see her stay. 'No,' says the girl. 'My young husband is waiting for me.'

She proceeded to sing the song through. A strange yelping song, mournful and repetitive but not without charm. She looked very pretty and knew it as she sang. I thought Mischa might be fed up about this performance but he was gazing at her in a dreamy sort of way, holding his glass and almost smiling. When she finished he said: 'That's what we like,' (he meant we Russians) 'to drink a bit and to sing.' 'If only', I couldn't help thinking 'you Russians would stick to that.'

'Money,' said Mischa, just like Sasha had said in Leningrad, 'is not a problem. You can have lots of money and live very poorly or a little and live well.'

There were conflicting interests between the workers and the intellectuals. The workers wanted a higher standard of living. The intellectuals would settle for more freedom just for starters. It was difficult for them to make common cause.

I mentioned opposition to the system. Mischa said every man woman and child was in opposition to the system.

'That's not what I mean,' I said. 'They are trying to cheat the system, or make it work for them. By opposition I mean people trying to change the system.'

'No one knows how to do that,' he said.

There is always a kind of gulf between foreigners, even if they share a language; but the gulf that separated us from Mischa was bottomless and alarming. I felt all the time with him, although he mellowed with drink and music, that he was feeling very wary. Perhaps he just thought we were boring, perhaps he didn't like Vera bringing home friends of her no-good sister, perhaps I misread him entirely and he was having a ball — I don't know. Somehow or other he made me uneasy.

'Have some more,' said Vera filling her glass for the fourth time. I was nursing mine along. 'No thanks,' I said.

'Why not?'

'Because I've got enough.' She looked at me for a moment. 'You haven't got a Russian character,' she said.

'Thank Christ,' I thought.

She did not make me feel uneasy. She was a familiar enough girl. Flirty and pretty, intelligent and wayward. She was about twenty-eight and already married and divorced twice. She was a bit wild and reckless and cared a lot about her career. She asked could I draw her — it was her dream to have her portrait done. The only time she'd sat for a painter friend she'd been livid at what he had done.

'I looked so old,' she complained.

'I could draw you but it would take ages and you'd have to sit very still.'

'I can't sit still. I never can. It's a problem. I can't even sit still for photographs, and I need good photographs for my work.'

I tried to remember her striking features to do a drawing of her later. If I did a good one I'd give it to her tomorrow. Harry had fixed to meet them again the next night to see another friend.

Mischa asked me if I'd like to meet some of his painter friends tomorrow and I said that I would very much. I was very surprised he should unbend so far as to suggest it.

We said we must go. It was very late and they both had to work tomorrow.

When she shook hands to say goodbye Vera curtsied.

Mischa came out with us to flag down a car. Several stopped but drove on after brief negotiations; then a taxi came. He wasn't allowed to stop, because taxis are supposed to wait at taxi ranks I think, but he took us anyway.

'See you tomorrow,' said Mischa. The taxi drove back to the hotel at about a million miles an hour.

Tuesday 13 October

First thing in the morning we rang Nigel. He had had no word from Warsaw. He suggested trying the British Embassy to see if they couldn't ask the Poles to do me a favour. But he didn't think it would do much good. I was beginning to realize things were getting a little tight. I was going to have to fix an alternative plan for leaving or at 4.00 tomorrow afternoon I was going to be in a bit of a spot.

On the other hand we had things to do today so we got on with them. I wanted to see the Tretyakov Museum where Russian painting was collected. It was interesting for two reasons. One was the work of the nineteenth-century painter Repin. Not that his work is all that terrific but it has a sort of power and skill which makes it outstanding and I know a few of the pictures from reproductions. The second reason was the propaganda pictures. There was an appalling work showing young Brezhnev in uniform greeting some soldiers somewhere in Russia during the war. In the picture he looked heroic and dashing and it was embarrassingly flattering. There was also a head carved in stone of Brezhnev looking keen, tough and vigorous. Both works were huge and violently ugly. There were also scenes of workers working or at play and grinning from ear to ear. Muscular, healthy, and happy, they looked so different from actual life as she is lived in this most peculiar country. Some of the war scenes were just like our pictures in the same genre — but in this lot of modern pictures artistic merit seemed missing to me. It was very hard to retain any sort of critical faculty when one already had such strong anti-feelings about the whole school. But I would put our war artists streets ahead of these guys for sheer variety and artistic ambition if nothing else. I mean our lot tried out techniques and explored avant-garde styles with plenty of elan and high spirits which was lacking in the Russian pictures.

Nevertheless there was a great deal to enjoy in the gallery and I was very glad to have gone. I liked a portrait of Turgenev, looking sleepy and gentle.

We had to return to the hotel in a hurry to meet Ivan, a friend of Harry's who had arranged to take us to lunch at a restaurant 20 kilometres outside Moscow. We splashed back through pouring rain trying vainly to stop a car to take us. Perhaps we looked too foreign, perhaps we did it wrong — I don't know. No one stopped.

Ivan was waiting outside the hotel. Thin and intense, with a haggard look and occasional brilliant smile, he was the most interesting of the Russians we met. Harry had known him for some time and said he was the only Russian he had ever met with whom he could speak quite openly and frankly.

Before we left for the restaurant we rang Nigel — still no message from Warsaw about my visa. We decided to call at the British Embassy on our way out of Moscow to ask for help. We asked Ivan, who spoke fluent English, whether we could call there on our way to the restaurant. Harry was anxious about Ivan taking us to the Embassy. He asked whether Ivan minded taking the risk. Ivan replied, no he didn't mind. He said he'd see when we got to the Embassy. If there were too many police who looked too interested he might park round the corner so that they wouldn't note down his number. I got the impression that Harry was slightly more worried about all this than Ivan, who said that he had let someone know that his old friend Harry was in town and that they were going to lunch together. This openness to a certain extent protected him. The word had not come back 'don't'.

I found it terribly difficult to keep in my mind that this sort of cloak and dagger behaviour was deadly serious and very necessary for the Russians — and for Harry, who understood it far better than I. If you went to Russia and never spoke to a Russian there was no reason why you should ever sense that it was going on — even I with all the contacts I made through Harry had to keep on being reminded.

Throughout this afternoon that we spent with Ivan he frequently dropped his voice to a whisper or spoke from behind his hand or avoided mentioning a name — all, I came to the conclusion, out of habit as it sometimes happened when there really couldn't be anyone listening in. Once or twice, even after telling us a little joke, when he noticed me taking a note he would say gently laying his hand on my arm: 'You won't mention my name will you?' He did this for example after this little exchange.

ME: 'Was there a particular architect who was responsible for the Stalinsque skyscrapers in Moscow?'

IVAN: 'No — I don't think so.'

ME: 'There was no Albert Speer?'

IVAN: 'No — a committee, probably a team.'

ME: 'I see — they are horrible aren't they?'

IVAN: 'Yes — very ugly — do you know what we call this style of architecture?'

ME: 'No.'

IVAN: (lowering his voice) 'Repressionist!'

ME: (laughing and jotting it down).

IVAN: 'You won't mention my name will you?'

It crossed my mind several times that he was joking with me but both he and Harry remained straight-faced about it, and I came to the conclusion that it was serious. We passed a new building — some sort of trade centre I believe. Nigel had pointed it out as an example of quite good modern building. 'It's shaped rather like an open book,' he had remarked.

'Yes,' replied Harry 'and the symbology ends there!'

Ivan chattered on about life in Moscow. He had lived and worked in the West and was quite well paid I gathered. It was a crime, a stupid wicked crime, that any man, let alone an intelligent and useful one as he was should live such a curtailed and limited life. Told what he could read and what was forbidden, where he might go and where he might not, and whom he might contact.

At the Embassy Ivan simply stopped the car and waited. Two police guards looked at him but barely seemed to take any notice.

We walked in, and at the gate had to show our passports. As I took mine out I realized with a blush of embarrassment that here I was a New Zealander, as I was travelling on my New Zealand passport. What a ridiculous situation. However they let me in and the official on the desk let me telephone the New Zealand consul. I got through to a very helpful secretary who said call back at 2.30 p.m. I asked her to ask the consul could he please phone the Polish Embassy and ask them either to hurry up and give me a visa or issue at least a transit visa so that I could either go on with Harry to Vienna where he lived, or simply switch to my train from Warsaw to London. She said she'd try.

We drove on out through the suburbs of Moscow. I asked what people thought about the Government slogans put up on banners and hoardings and rooftops all over Russia. Ivan replied people thought of them, if they thought of them at all, as a bad joke. Harry wondered what effect they had on people's thinking and attitudes. I thought probably quite a considerable effect. If they had been there all your life and always repeated endlessly the same message — no matter how idiotic it was it must somewhere lodge in you. Ivan didn't agree. He shrugged. To him they were absurd. He couldn't imagine anyone ever took the slightest notice of them.

He said Mitterand's victory was a grave blow for the Soviet Government. We expressed amazement. Socialist Government in France, Communist Ministers appointed in the West. Surely the Politburo must be laughing. On the contrary, insisted Ivan it was extremely embarrassing for them. They had to report it, because they had to keep friendly with the French but how the devil did they tell the Russians that Communists had been elected to office in the West? Democracy worked and that could not be. It amused Ivan to see *Pravda* trying to deal with this pesky problem.

As we went down the highway we passed many policemen, sometimes just standing by the road, once in the middle of the road, sometimes in roadside shelters. Ivan explained that they could radio ahead to the next policeman to keep the centre lane open if some big torpedo was coming through in his Zill, and to stop up any side roads or prevent turning vehicles from getting in its way. The police also could arbitrarily set up check-points down this road and there were usually two at night on the route we travelled. They stopped you, asked where you were headed and where you had been — that was all.

Ivan said he had been driving back the other night and near where we were he had passed a factory — it was all dark, as it was the middle of the night, except for a huge neon portrait of Lenin. When he saw it he laughed so much and so hard that he nearly drove straight off the road. Someone had suspended light bulbs where Lenin's eyes were, giving the head a mad startled expression. Even remembering it he began chuckling and giggling again and it occurred to me that although I'm sure it was funny perhaps it wasn't *that* funny and in his merriment was a touch of the schoolboy laughing in church, the humour growing out of the fact that it was something you simply mustn't laugh at.

Harry asked him if in his academic capacity he ever had to mark the exam papers of the children of high-ups in the Party and if so was he told to give them good marks no matter what they deserved.

Ivan replied 'Yes,' meaning yes to both questions. He went on to say that in those circumstances he simply refused to examine those students, or I rather gathered somehow passed the dirty job on to someone else. He illustrated this situation with a joke. He knew lots of these little stories and often used them to illustrate or sum up whatever it was we were talking about.

The son of a high official was being examined in anatomy. He was shown a skeleton, tall, with a small head, narrow hips and big hands and feet and asked to comment on what could be learnt from it. He couldn't think of anything. He was shown a second skeleton not so tall, small head, wide hips, small hands and feet. Still he could think of nothing one could say about it. He was shown a third skeleton. Much smaller than the other two, large head, small hips, small hands and feet. Still an utter blank. Exasperated, the examiner muttered: 'Didn't they manage to teach you *anything* at medical school?' 'Oh,' said the student. 'I see what you mean — the skeletons are of Marx, Engels, and Lenin!' Ivan actually whispered the punch line.

You could see the use of these jokes to Russians and why the authorities disapproved of them.

He described how unbelievably complicated life was for a Russian citizen. Nothing could just be done. Everything was achieved through having influence, or being lucky enough to know someone who knew someone. A sequence of good turns was necessary no matter how ordinary the thing you wanted. It might be theatre tickets, a spare part for your car, some paint or a bit of cloth. He knew someone who spent six months looking for a right-hand bumper for his car. In the end he found a left-hand bumper and bought it anyway in case he could swap it for a right-hand one later somewhere else.

At one point in the afternoon Harry asked was there anything he could send Ivan from Austria. Ivan said there was. He had heard you could buy bits of clear cellophane or plastic so marked that if you stuck one of them on your windscreen it appeared to be cracked. He wanted one of these children's novelty jokes to discourage thieves from swiping his windscreen — a fashion that was growing here because of shortages.

Money, he said, was not a problem. Many Russians had told us so. People had plenty of money — what they lacked was anything to spend it on. He said he was on a waiting list for a new car. He must wait at least one, maybe two years. The price of the new car was fixed and he could more or less pay for it by selling the six– or seven-year-old heap he was driving at the moment. As soon as the new car arrived he would put his name down for another new car which would, with luck, get to him before his first new one packed up. What a system! He told us about how you set about getting asked to join the Communist Party. You did as much social work as you could. This turned out to be youth work or trade union work or helping local old people and so on. 'Being a druzhinnik?' I asked. 'Yes — of course,' he replied. 'That sort of thing.' This work would take up literally all your spare time. He couldn't be bothered to do it although I gathered he had at times considered trying to join for the benefits that would follow.

'Do you have to keep up this work after you are asked to join?' I asked.

'Yes,' he replied. 'Oh yes you do.' Then with a smile: 'For a bit anyway.'

I didn't begin to understand how it worked but if you worked hard enough you got to be a party member. If you were a party member life became easier for you. So you worked hard at being a good Communist so that you and your family could enjoy your party privileges.

The restaurant was called The Russian House and was built to look like a traditonal log building. Inside it was all wood and carved pillars and panels. Really very nice. It was almost empty both downstairs and up and Ivan explained it was usually fuller in the evening. A man and a woman sat at one table. Young middle-aged, it was difficult to see what their relationship was. Nearby six men talked and laughed together quietly. We saw quite a quantity of vodka going to their table. Ivan thought they could be wealthy salesmen having a business lunch.

An unbelievably rude waiter took our order. Ivan ordering for all of us. The waiter, tall and bronzed wearing a Russian embroidered shirt and sash looked, apart from his costume, like an advert for a Nazi health camp. He had those hideous good looks that the Nazis favoured in their young soldiers. Pale eyes, strong jaw and sensual curved lips. Absolute shit he was — resting his weight on one leg, sighing and frowning and

tapping his pencil while Ivan thought. Then when Ivan ordered something he would repeat it with insolent incredulity as if to say 'Kvass? You want kvass? Oh my God! He wants kvass now.' At last this swine went away and I said to Ivan that he was the most rude and generally unbearable waiter I'd ever seen. Ivan smiled and pointed: 'Him?' he said. 'No — really?' 'Wasn't he being rude?' I asked. 'All that sighing and barking and carrying on?' Ivan said, yes he was rude all right, but on the scale he was used to that wasn't too bad. 'He was just a lousy waiter. But what could you do?' He seemed genuinely not to care. The creep would bring the food so — who cared.

The creep did bring the food and the wine and it was very good indeed. I cannot remember all the dishes, there were so many. Mushrooms, fish, salads, meat, side dishes of cheese and sausage, black bread and lovely butter. The meal meandered on. Several times I thought it was finished but half-an-hour later another plate would arrive and be slowly consumed. Outside the weather was turning worse; rain lashed down and the wind roared. Inside it was lazy and quiet. We kind of drifted through the afternoon.

Once Ivan took me downstairs to ring the New Zealand consul. The phone was out of order so we drove a quarter of a mile to the Post Office in the village and I telephoned from there. I was delighted to find myself in this, to me, Chekhovian setting; full of Russian food, my feet squelching on muddy Russian roads, I was living out a fantasy I had often indulged in.

The quiet reassuring voice of Mr Dayken, (I don't know how you spell it) brought a rush of nostalgic affection for my adopted country. He said he'd done what he could and would ring again later to shake them up but it was really a matter of luck. It'd probably be all right in the end. We would probably be able to fix a tourist visa anyway. . . . I left the phone box full of affection for Mr Dayken — and Ivan and I returned to the restaurant.

At about 4.30 p.m. Ivan paid for our meal. He insisted that we should not contribute. It had been absolutely wonderful — in trying to describe the conversation I have quite failed to get across the lazy meandering charm of this way of eating. Food casually and unexpectedly arriving, being consumed and replaced with other dishes — the wine and kvass, the slow feeling of an afternoon stretching pleasantly before and behind one — it was delightful.

Back in the car Ivan drove off in the same direction by which we'd arrived.

'Where are we going?' said Harry.

'A different route back,' said Ivan.

The road wound through the wooded countryside and soon we were going along an exceptionally pretty and well kept section which was really what Ivan wanted to show us. Every two hundred yards or so, perhaps less frequently, there were turnings off this quiet road. Each turning had a 'no entry' sign, some had policemen guarding them. Down these enticing little roads that turned and vanished into the beech trees were the beautiful dachas of the rulers of Russia. The ultra-privileged Politburo chiefs who never met the people, who lived utterly private, isolated lives, and appeared now and then like Zombies on the repulsive mausoleum in Red Square to watch ICBMs dragged by. Here they holed up, screeching down the centre lane of the highway to the Kremlin and back, occasionally murdering each other. The biggest time crooks in the world. I don't think most Russians have the foggiest idea how these sinister men live. How could they? It was creepy driving through their turf. Here and there through the trees you could glimpse beautifully painted fences, looking unusually spick and span in this jerry-built, decaying country. Ivan pointed to one brick dacha that was right by the road.

'That was one of Stalin's,' he said. He may have said, 'so I've been told', or 'so they say.' as well, I didn't quite catch his words.

We returned to the highroad back to town. 'Here,' he said, 'you can see Brezhnev driving to town early each morning.' He described a huge motorcade, multi-coloured lights flashing, outrider cars weaving to and fro to press back ordinary traffic. I wish I could have seen it.

It was getting dark as we got back to town. Harry wanted to go to the large hard-currency shop to buy something or other and he asked to be taken there. It was quite interesting — for a start, at the door a porter made as if to stop Harry entering because he was speaking Russian to Ivan. 'Speak English! speak English,' hissed Ivan and the man stepped back as Harry snapped into his native tongue. Inside there was no queue anywhere — the shelves were heavily laden with all kinds of goods and plenty of them. The shoppers were German and Scandinavian as far as I could see, and us, but there were not many people about.

Harry bought Ivan a bottle of Grand Marnier and said 'What else can we get you? Name it — something for your wife? Your son?' Ivan was insistent. 'Please,' he said, 'don't worry — it's no problem — no, no, nothing.'

I bought some books. One on the Hermitage that I hadn't seen at the Hermitage bookstall. Even here you could not browse through the books as you could anywhere in the West. You had to point to anything you were interested in and get it handed to you for a quick look. It made shopping very tiresome.

Ivan looked around this capsule of forbidden plenty right in the heart of his city.

'See.' he said very bitterly. 'They can make it work when they want to.' I felt embarrassed. It was humiliating and painful suddenly, to be handing him goodies that we could easily afford on our western incomes and expense accounts, when we were in his town, and in a shop he wasn't really supposed to enter.

Through him I felt something of the horror of living in this cruel, stupid and inefficient system. 'When something goes wrong, never, never try to find out why,' he said, 'because you'll never get an answer.'

I asked Harry whether Ivan had ever said he'd like, or might like to live in the West. Harry was shocked: 'No, no, never,' he said sharply. 'He never would. It's the one thing you *never* discuss — not with anyone. It's dynamite. It's far too dangerous.'

Back in the hotel we looked forward to seeing Vera and Mischa. The arrangement was they would call us at 6.00 p.m. We waited in Harry's room. We waited and waited but no call came. After three-quarters of an hour Harry left the hotel to call their flat — but there was no reply. Once more we felt the familiar uncertainty — a clammy fog had come down. What had happened — why hadn't they rung? Had they been told not to — had Mischa decided it was unwise — was there some perfectly simply explanation we had overlooked, a misunderstanding? We never found out.

Under the door in my room was a message from Lennie Hoffmann. It said he was having dinner upstairs in our hotel with some colleagues. We went to find them. They were in a restaurant on the fourth floor. A very different place to the noisy naughty restaurant downstairs. Here it was a hard-currency restaurant, staid and quiet, with dinner jacketed waiters and American Express and Visa card signs on the door. It was fun meeting Lennie in such an unlikely place. His friends were very English lawyery. One was really uptight with a prim little mouth and disapproving manner — the other two were more riotous and silly and engaging. They had all visited Moscow several times (except Len) and their delight (the second two) was to go to the hard-currency bar having first discovered something that was out of stock, and waving fistsful of dollars demand to be served it. The general disquiet this behaviour produced endlessly entertained them.

'It really bugs them!'

'They don't like it at all!'

We all moved down to the noisy restaurant — much more fun. Here, while Harry began a furious row with the waiter, I talked to Lennie. As I babbled on about the things I had seen and done I realized I was completely high. Not on alcohol — I hadn't had any since hours before at lunch — just from being here. I was longing to just unload everything I had seen and heard. I was hardly making sense.

Harry's row was about the tablecloth. He had asked for it to be changed. The waiter said or seemed to be saying 'shove off! If you don't like the tablecloth go somewhere else.' He was gesticulating and angry. Later Harry came to the conclusion that in fact he was saying: 'All right but first you must get up so that I can get to it and re-lay the table,' which eventually is what happened. Lennie and his friends had already had dinner, but we ordered caviare and smoked salmon, vodka and lemonade — that is all except the school-mistressy one. He had a cup of coffee. We had a very giggly and enjoyable dinner, shouting above the noise of the band and knocking back shots of vodka. Finally, we agreed to walk together to the National Hotel to see Lennie's room.

It was a clear night and only a five-minute walk. As we went Lennie's two friends told me about how they were mugged or rather robbed in a pedestrian underpass nearby. Two young men came up to them in a friendly boisterous way asking them to sell their coats. The two Englishmen said 'no'. The Russians became more insistent and grabbed at the lapels of one of the lawyers and shook it — a certain amount of jostling took place and then the Russians left — and the lawyer found his wallet and pens gone. They told the police, who were very shocked and promised Moscow would be combed, no stone left unturned, etc. But nothing came of it.

I thought the Metropole was pretty good in its way but it could not hold a candle to the National. It was here that Lenin stayed when he first returned to Moscow, so Lennie told me. It seemed to date from the 1890s because the decoration was all art nouveau, with dreamy girls' heads and twisting leaves and flowers, carved into banisters, walls and pillars. Lennie's room, or rather suite, had a balcony and from it we looked across a broad street to the Kremlin above whose spotlit spires rode a full moon. It was a superb sight, both beautiful and sinister. I stood and gazed until I was full of it.

Harry and I walked back to the Metropole with Lennie's two wilder colleagues. They wanted to go and annoy the staff in the hard-currency bar. On the way back we passed a young woman. She was standing on a pavement by the entrance to a pedestrian subway. Her hands were in her pockets, and she half turned to look at us with a strange blank expression. She was urinating. It was a very surprising sight. There were a number of people about and it took me a moment to realize where the splashing trickle of water she was standing in came from. In fact I didn't really believe my eyes. After we had gone on a little way I said:

'That girl — she was peeing.'

'Which girl?' said Harry.

'Where?' said one young lawyer.

'Yes — she was,' said the other lawyer.

90

Wednesday 14 October

I had breakfast alone, served by a rude and irritated-looking waitress. This was more like I had been told service was like. Without Harry's presence to protect me the girl bullied me mercilessly and I disliked her very much, as she muttered away in Russian tapping her pencil and pulling faces.

Before setting off for a last desperate attempt to get my Polish visa Harry rang the Embassy to ask whether it had arrived. I could tell straight away without needing a translation that it had and I felt very pleased and happy. Nigel lent us his car and driver and we went to pick it

up. I didn't mention that on our last visit to the Embassy a few days before there were several Arabs also waiting to pick up visas. Today there were more. I was conscious of being irritated by their presence and was puzzled about why I should feel such antagonism towards them. I had mentioned it to Harry and we came to the conclusion that somewhere subliminally we connected all the black and Arab people we saw with black and Arab Moscow-trained terrorists, guerrillas and revolutionaries that we had read about so often in our newspapers. After coming to this conclusion every time I saw a coloured man I pictured him waving his Kalashnikov or wearing battledress and haranguing a crowd. It intrigued me that I should have such violent fantasies here because I don't remember ever having had such feelings about similar men in England.

Once having got the visa safely in my pocket I was eager to leave

91

Moscow. I was already beginning to find this city oppressive. Leningrad became more and more beautiful and full of charm in my mind's eye with every day I spent in Moscow. In a small way I felt we had immediately got into Leningrad but had remained bouncing on the surface of Moscow and I'm afraid that even after such a short stay I was not sorry we were going. I was very keen to visit the Pushkin Museum before we left, if for no other reason because there is housed the only painting Van Gogh ever sold, *The Red Vineyard*, and I wanted to see it — to pay my respects to it, if you can to a painting.

Back we went through Moscow, the driver going very fast and sending up sheets of spray from the flooded roads. The Russians don't seem to have mastered the trick of draining roads and pavements — a drop of rain and soon puddles are linking up and forming small lakes, cars have the look of motor boats, and you can get drowned waiting to cross the road in the tidal waves thrown up by buses and lorries.

The Pushkin had many fine paintings and as usual I enjoyed the paintings but the nineteenth-century collection was not available to see. These galleries were closed and many of the pictures out on loan. I was disappointed.

Ivan had arranged to take us to the station to catch the Warsaw train and we had a last lunch at the Metropole while we waited for him. He arrived with his girl-friend in time for coffee. She didn't speak English and I couldn't tell much about her. She had a funny Russian smile, at least I think of it as a Russian smile, that crinkled up her eyes and showed all her upper teeth and gums. She was quite pretty and very quiet.

On the way to the station we drove past the Lubianka once more.

'Do you know what that building was before the Revolution?' asked Ivan.

'No, what?'

'An insurance company's office.'

'Still is a sort of insurance office, I suppose,' said Harry, looking at its bland facade. Its very ordinaryness seems to make it fifty times more sinister. Horrible place. Having destroyed the mausoleum and sent home the queue to see Lenin the Russians could do worse than pull down the Lubianka — or perhaps empty it of torturers, interviewers, and secret police and throw it open to the public as a grisly museum — as a warning of what can happen if police and government get too powerful.

A remark of Ivan's just came back to me. I can't remember whether I had jotted it down. We were talking about the people waiting in their endless line to see Lenin, and he said bitterly and contemptuously: 'They wait, for hours and hours to see "the doll".' Lenin's body, once on show, has long since been replaced by a wax model. It's so bloody silly.

92

Ivan and his girl-friend waited round the corner from Nigel's flat. They did not want to come in and say hello — neither I rather gathered were they too keen to be seen by the police guard who occupied a sentry-box at the gateway to the 'compound'.

We said goodbye and thanks to Nigel and Chris and left them in their large flat. They were being photographed by a friend and said cheerily: 'See you in London!'

We returned to the car and were soon at the station. Ivan insisted on carrying my heavy bag. He looked so thin and frail that I tried first to take it from him and then to at least share it, but he wouldn't hear of it.

Our compartment was clean and roomy — just like the train that had taken me from Helsinki to Leningrad.

We said goodbye to Ivan and his girl-friend at the station. He shook hands warmly taking my hand in both of his. Harry said he hoped they'd meet in the West soon. Ivan had mentioned the possibility of another trip abroad. I said how very much pleasure it would give me to meet him in London if he was ever passing through.

He smiled and said that would be great. London, he had told us at lunch, was his favourite foreign city.

When the train pulled out I was very aware of how different it was saying goodbye to Ivan and saying au revoir to Nigel. The sense of relief I had to be quitting Moscow and Russia was tinged with pity to be leaving Ivan almost like a prisoner in his own country.

I ought to say I am prone to these rather romantic thoughts — there was nothing in Ivan's manner to make me think such things — and as for my relief at quitting Moscow, that was also because I was now on my way home, and I'm not too happy away from my family for too long — but even so. . . .

While Harry slept I watched the flat Russian landscape speeding past. There was very little to see. Damp, autumn forest, or prairie stretching away for ever. Now and then villages and empty roads.

We went to have something to eat at about 7.00. The restaurant car was quite full, mostly with workers. Harry said they were Polish and guessed they were going home on leave after a stint doing some specialized work in Russia. Some were getting drunk, one was being gently restrained by a huge companion. I don't know what he wanted to do but he allowed himself to be pushed back into his seat — didn't have much choice actually. Among the Poles was one Russian. He had a round tummy and wore spectacles and he was arguing with a table-full of Poles. The conversation was rowdy but good-natured. Often the Russian would rest his arm on the shoulder of one of the men he was talking to or a Pole would tap the Russian gently on the hand to emphasize a point. They swapped cigarettes and gave each other lights.

Harry couldn't hear everything that was being said but the conversation turned in part on whether Russia was a benign and good friend to all the world or not. At one point several of the Poles got up and left, looking bored by the Russian's insistent arguing. The rest soon fell silent and then they too got up and went — one of them embracing the Russian in a friendly way before leaving the restaurant.

Meanwhile we ordered eggs, cheese, bread and wine from the old lady serving in the restaurant car. Others were eating a kind of stew and vegetables and yet others sausages. There was quite a good choice. The tables were clean and the wine good. After the cheese and eggs she brought us tea and some pretty terrible cakes. We ate this while listening to the Poles and Russian arguing.

'You can't argue with Russians,' said Harry. 'You must either say "Yes! Yes! Yes!" to everything or right from the start tell them "You are ruled by criminals . . . *Everything* they tell you is a lie . . . nothing they promise will happen and their inefficiency is obvious to everything they attempt. They are greedy, bullies and hypocrites and the idea that they are building a better society, or working for peace and freedom, would be laughable if it wasn't so utterly stupid." '

Soon Harry started chatting to the old lady. She told him about the war. The Germans, whom she hated, had overrun her village and occupied it for about six months. She had two small children and her husband had been killed in action in 1941. The Germans killed all the livestock — pigs, cows, horses, chickens, everything — and before they left they burned the village to the ground. It had been a 'difficult' time. I looked at her ugly old face. Her grey hair was drawn into a bun — she smiled a lot and patted Harry's arm as she spoke to him. I hoped she had found another man. I noticed she wore a wedding ring and soon she mentioned that her youngest son was born after the war, and I felt pleased. It was noticeable how many elderly women worked in the Soviet Union — as waitresses, seamstresses, as caretakers or whatever you call them in art galleries, guards in railway or underground stations and so on. She was a very nice old lady. Before we left she and the kitchen staff came and sat down and had their supper. . . .

I didn't sleep too well — I never do on trains. I was feeling a little worried about my notebooks — dreading them being confiscated. The compartment was chilly.

POLAND

Thursday 15 October

At about 5.30 a.m. we got to the Polish border and the guards and customs men came through the train. They looked carefully at the photograph in my passport and then at me, once sure that I was carrying *my* passport. They asked how many articles of baggage I had. 'Three,' I said. And Harry? 'Two,' he said. They nodded and went out. That was the end of the customs check. I was just relieved but Harry was intrigued. 'Why?' he wanted to know. He kept saying that they always give you more of a search than that. Had some word come through not to search our luggage? Had some Russian figured it was in their interest for Harry or for me, a *Telegraph* journalist, to have a good impression of their country? Or was it once more just luck — just chance that we picked two easy-going guards. One way or the other I didn't care.

The Poles who got in next were cheerful, merry young men who when they saw my New Zealand passport asked me something I didn't understand.

'What are they saying?' I asked Harry.

'They are asking if you know someone called ------.' (I've forgotten the name.)

'No,' I said, 'I don't.'

The two young men looked incredulous and made strange gestures and roaring noises. Harry laughed.

'He is a famous New Zealand motor-cycling champion,' he said. 'They cannot believe a New Zealander wouldn't know his name. They've rumbled you — you've had it,' he said.

The Poles left, laughing and shaking their heads. Again it was, I suppose just luck, but this little exchange had such a different flavour to that created by the polite but stern Russians.

Outside, as dawn broke, even the countryside of Poland looked more friendly than the flat plains of Russia. Here there were wooded slopes and smaller fields. We saw several farmers walking across their fields with one cow and were puzzled. Why only one? 'More means capitalism, probably,' said Harry. We also saw quite a few horse-drawn carts and at least once a man ploughing with a team of horse. 'No petrol — perhaps no machinery,' said Harry.

I was aware of a lightening of my spirits. To be in Poland was not the same as being in the USSR. Here was Solidarity and the atmosphere of struggle and reform.

The railway station at Warsaw looked clean and tidy and modern. You moved smoothly from one level to another on shiny escalators and the people thronging the place looked more cheerful, more brightly dressed and more purposeful than I had grown used to Russians looking. This kind of judgement or perception was very untrustworthy. Obviously one's attitude to the Poles was so different to one's attitude to the Russians that what you 'saw' could not be all that objective — but it seemed to me right from the start that the very air was lighter.

Outside the station the air actually was 'lighter'. It had been pouring with rain in Moscow — here brilliant sunshine glowed on the buildings and streets. The sky was clear and blue.

I waited in line for a taxi while Harry left his suitcases. He was catching a late afternoon train home and we planned to go to my hotel, wash, shave and then spend the day with some old friends of Harry's who lived not far from the centre of the city. While I waited a middle-aged, well dressed woman spoke to me. I said in English: 'I'm sorry, I do not speak Polish.' She spoke again, this time in French, and made a little joke about the weather being so fine here and so rotten in Moscow. As we chatted about nothing I felt an even greater lightening of my mood. Here people spoke French — or at least some did. In Russia for me it had been English or nothing, and I felt less helpless as I realized my chances of being able to communicate had just doubled. (In fact, though my French is a shameful mess, I used it three or four times in Poland and although it must have been an unpleasant experience for the Poles, it helped deal with the feeling that I had lost my brain which comes from being in a country where you speak no word of the language.)

The taxi driver when he came at once asked if we wanted to change money. I had some dollars and Harry asked what price the driver was offering. It was three times the official rate and, as Harry told me to, I changed a few dollars. It seemed to me I was given an awful lot of zlotys. The driver took my dollars saying in a pained voice and shrugging — 'Why change so few?'

The hotel, a brand new one, built by Swedes, so I was told, was like any Euro hotel. Signs in English, Polish, German, etc . . . staff speaking very good English, comfortable room with bath, TV, phone, radio, fridge and so on. Much refreshed by baths, shaves and coffee, and after Harry had made a few phone calls (now speaking fluent Polish by the way) we walked to the Palace of Culture. Built just after the war by the Russians, this architectural nightmare in Stalin's 'repressionist' style dominated the city. It was so vast, so tall, so hideous you understood as soon as you clapped eyes on it what an enormous task Solidarity had taken on. To shift the system that built things like that was a frightening proposition. . . .

On the twenty-third floor of this 'present from the Russian people' we visited Harry's friend — a distinguished member of the scientific establishment. He was not sitting in his office but in a little conference room nearby because the heating was not working and the conference room was warmed by the sunshine.

He spoke very good English and I had been in his company for at least five minutes when I suddenly realized we were talking absolutely freely without even thinking about bugging or reporting or not mentioning names and all that sort of nastiness you got so used to in Russia. I don't mean you never had this sort of conversation in Russia but there you became possessed by a kind of latent paranoia. Your first instinct was to be guarded in case you endangered or embarrassed your companions as much as for any fear for yourself.

Chatting in this man's office one could have been in the West and once more I felt that raising of my spirits.

He was 'optimistic' about the future of Poland. He felt that after three decades of mistakes and mismanagement they were on the right track at last. Solidarity would be criticized for tactical mistakes or for mistiming gestures but fundamentally they were right. He did not expect a Russian military intervention and never had done. He did believe they would try every other sort of pressure they could think of, but this was a Polish problem and the Poles would see it through. He thought the West had judged the whole thing very well and reacted absolutely correctly right from the start. They had been firm and clear in their support for the proposed reforms and yet had avoided being tactless and provocative. He said the task facing his country was enormous; he was very worried about the winter — energy and food shortages would create terrible hardships during the cold weather — 'but it had been a good summer.'

He looked forward to seeing Harry soon in the West at a conference they would both be attending.

As I left his office I was feeling positively euphoric. He had given me a feeling of tremendous optimism and hope. I was really very surprised by his smiling confidence and relaxed facing up to the problems ahead.

The next few days involved me in a quick and radical reassessment of this cheery view — and a more solemn, realistic, and grim sort of pessimism gradually overcame me. I never came to believe their battle was hopeless but that they were nowhere near as far advanced as at first I had wildly hoped. They had, in fact, merely reached the end of the beginning and they faced great hardships for a long long time. But it was hardship touched at least with moments of passionate excitement and, I hope it is not too fanciful to say, sometimes almost carnival mood of being on the move — even though the journey was so perilous and the ultimate destination uncertain.

After half an hour of this encouraging conversation Harry and I left to visit his other friends. We went by tram. As we crossed the centre of Warsaw I was struck by a peculiar quality or atmosphere the city had. It took me a while to work out what it could be. I think I understood it in the end and during the days I was there the feeling of strangeness grew rather than faded. I came to the conclusion that this sensation of something being 'wrong' originated in the knowledge that everything we were looking at was either a rebuilt or a new building. One was used in Europe to seeing centuries piled one on top of the other, or, higgledy piggledy, existing side by side in a curiously comforting and pleasant mess, but in Warsaw the Nazis interrupted this development and razed the city to the ground. The rebuilding, done at various times by different authorities with very different aims, had produced a kind of architectural incoherence. The streets were sometimes far too wide, the high-rise housing blocks too near the centre, the juxtaposition of ugly modern styles with lovingly reconstructed ancient buildings, oddly sad and depressing. It all had the effect of bringing the war and the post-war occupation of Poland very close, and you were slowly forced to realize that to survive and to continue did not necessarily mean to recover from your wounds. The profound and enduring horror of the war was, so it seemed to me, very much alive below the surface in Warsaw. The damage was too great. A terrible ugliness was born.

But I was still in a cheerful mood, and Harry told me how he had met the family we were going to visit. While still at Cambridge in the fifties he had met a girl in a cinema queue. In the course of conversation he'd said he was going to visit Poland soon and she had given him the address of some relatives in Warsaw. She had insisted he should visit them and said she'd write and tell them he was coming. Some weeks later he'd turned up at the very flat we were now heading for. He had knocked on the door and it had been opened by an elderly man. When Harry introduced himself the old man had been mystified. Somewhat disconcerted Harry asked: 'But didn't so-and-so tell you I was arriving?' 'No,' replied the old man, 'she didn't — but come in, come in. How long would you like to stay?' Harry had become a close friend of the family ever since and I was touched by the affectionate way he was greeted by the old lady who opened the door to us. She was the widow of the man Harry had first met twenty-five years before. They spoke in French so that I could follow the conversation, and first of all Harry gave her the presents he had brought her. Chocolate, coffee, tea, soap, and so on, all of which she accepted with expressions of pleasure — saving her most ecstatic reaction for a roll of aluminium foil and a roll of plastic cling wrap that Harry produced. She actually clasped her hands and gasped with delight. While her happiness was infectious, a distant note of anxiety was struck by the extraordinary reaction to this present. What kind of topsy turvy world were we actually in? I had been thinking that after Russia we were back in the West here — but were we?

The flat was in a pre-war block. That is to say presumably a rebuilt pre-war block. Just how much housing the Germans left standing I'm not certain — but this was a solid and attractive place with wooden parquet floors and quite large rooms. The old lady lived here with her daughter-in-law, a lawyer, and grandson aged sixteen. Her son lived and worked in Switzerland. The lawyer seemed to divide her time between Switzerland and Poland.

The old lady began at once to talk about life in Warsaw and straight away began to qualify the picture I'd got from the scientist half an hour earlier. She was extremely worried and pessimistic. She feared the winter very much. Because her daughter-in-law and young grandson lived with her she would be looked after, but for many others the immediate future was very alarming. An old lady in the next flat had fainted from hunger the other day, because by chance no one had visited her and the phone didn't work. . . .

In the sunny room, which was full of flowers and decorated with nineteenth-century family portraits, pretty glass and china and well furnished, it was hard to take in fully how serious her situation was. Although she was talking of her fears that 'civil war' might break out between the peasants and the urban workers; and that her grandson had said his schoolfellows had resolved that should the Russians invade they would take arms and fight; and that army conscripts in Cracow had sworn in the cathedral before going off on basic training that they would never fire on Poles — her manner was by no means gloomy or unhappy. She sounded energetic and robust and she frequently laughed and smiled. It often amused me the way elderly people talked about the absurd behaviour of even older people, when to me the difference in their ages or general condition was not that great. Rocking with laughter she told us that an aged friend of hers had taken down and unsheathed an antique cavalry sabre and, holding it in a frail hand, had declared that if the Russians came 'I am armed'. The comic side of the story was obvious but so was the tragic and frightening side.

Shortly after we arrived our hostess's daughter-in-law Zosia came in. She was about forty, very intense, and somewhat stern. She smiled rarely and when she did it was not a very warm or wide smile. She spoke only Polish and, while sounding more defiant than her mother-in-law, was if anything more pessimistic. However she felt in the end that the battle against the Polish Government and its Russian allies would be won: 'Because it *must* be won.' Several other Poles said to me during the next few days when I asked them about the future: 'Of course we are optimistic — what else can we be?'

Like all the Poles I spoke to she said the winter could be critical. She did not fear a military intervention from the Russians: 'They will rely on economic weapons.'

She believed that many desperately needed goods, including food, equipment and medical supplies, were simply being stolen by the Russians. She told stories of trains being opened by Solidarity members and found to be falsely marked and carrying Polish property away to Russia. She recounted the story of a transplant surgeon who could no longer buy drugs he needed from the States because the hospital had no more dollars. He tried to arrange for a shipment to be delivered anyway. In desperation he eventually wrote personally to the head of the drug manufacturer begging for help and was told a representative from the firm was coming to see him. When he arrived the American said: 'Now, what is the problem? We have sent you enough supplies to give every Pole in the country a transplant.' None of it had arrived. She believed it had all gone to Russia.

She said the support and encouragement from the West had been of inestimable value — the West Germans particularly had been incredibly generous. The Poles were being forced to rethink their hatred for the Germans in the light of the many acts of kindness and the flow of money to Solidarity from West Germany. For East Germans they retained ferocious hatred.

When the lawyer's son came home we had lunch. It was good and plentiful. What I didn't realize at the time, because I had not seen the queues, was that it probably took several hours to buy and the meat probably represented a largish part of the family's monthly ration.

We sat long into the afternoon talking and the conversation was almost entirely about Poland and her struggle. It was comfortable and warm in the pretty room. We drank coffee and brandy and I found that I had to continually remind myself that this was all in deadly earnest. This wasn't happening somewhere in safe, free Western Europe. Here there could be arrests and shooting and riots and tanks and hunger. The very ordinaryness of the afternoon and the room made the cruel stupidity of the Communist Government and its Russian masters more horrible and hateful and more of a threat to me. These people were like me, I thought, much more than the Russians were like me — and if this ghastly nightmare could happen to them in their country it could happen to me in mine.

We stayed too long and Harry suddenly realized his train was leaving very soon. We rushed out of the house after Harry was given a fond farewell. We then spent a slightly ridiculous hour trying to re-find the left luggage depot in the railway station to pick up Harry's luggage; then found his train went from a different station; then found there were simply no taxis — we were at one time running around in circles quite unable to decide what to do and departure time was getting close. Harry finally found a car — I'm not sure it was a taxi — and I threw him 400 zlotys and with no time to say goodbye to each other after our adventures he roared away into the dark. I felt very alone for a moment, alone that is except for four tins of salted herrings that I suddenly remembered Harry had left in the fridge of my hotel room.

There was another reason why I was not alone — I had the names, phone numbers and addresses of five families who lived in Warsaw. They had been given to me by a Polish friend in Canada who had also given me some chocolate, tinned food, coffee, tea, soap, shampoo and dried fruit to bring to Warsaw for her friends.

I went up to my hotel room and tried to screw up my courage to ring one of my Polish contacts. I felt very poignantly the loss of Harry. He would have actually looked forward to the task. For me it required a great effort. I cannot really explain this sensation. I didn't think of myself as being particularly shy and I don't as a rule find it very difficult to talk to people. Perhaps I was tired. The incredible excitement of the last ten days in Russia, a pretty sleepless night on the train, the brandy at lunch . . . I don't know.

I decided to ring Caroline first and found I could do that direct. I dialled the numbers and there she was. In two minutes I felt much revived. Home was OK, the children fine, and I would be leaving Warsaw in three-and-a-half days and would see them all again. When I hung up I immediately dialled the first Warsaw number I'd been given.

The phone was answered by Magda, a journalist married to Roman, a playwright, novelist and sometime famous young dissident writer. Magda said she was expecting me to call — how was I? When could we meet? What would I like to see? Had I spoken yet to anyone else? — and so on. We agreed to meet at 10.00 the following morning in the hotel lobby.

'I will probably wear an old American leather flying jacket,' she said. I wondered how to describe myself. 'I will wear a light-coloured wind-cheater; oh and I'll be carrying some notebooks in a khaki shoulder bag.'

I sat in the hotel room wondering what to do. It was about 8.00 p.m. I tried the TV set and watched the heads talking Polish for a few minutes. I tried writing up my journal. I felt tired and restless. . . . Then the phone rang. It was one of the people on my list. This was Ryczard. His English was not quite as good as Magda's but he was wonderfully friendly and welcoming. He said he'd ring again later tomorrow, that he hoped to meet me then and that he knew yet another friend was fixing up a meeting on Saturday.

I was beginning to feel a lot less alone and I went for a walk. I just wandered through the dark empty streets. A few cars passed by, and now and then a clump of people waited at a trolley-bus stop or walked the pavement like me. I vaguely knew where I was because from time to time I caught sight of the lights on top of the Palace of Culture. Then surprisingly they vanished. I turned a corner expecting to see the damned thing and it had gone. I pressed on in the same direction and was soon lost. I felt I could have probably retraced my way but was too proud to be so feeble so I went on.

There was not much to see, partly because the shops were either empty or quite dark and partly because this rebuilt city is short of the little architectural pleasures most big European cities have here and there, no matter how developed and rebuilt they are. I felt absolutely no fear or nervousness at being out in the streets in the dark. Once a drunk staggered towards me down the empty little street, but took no notice of me, and was anyway in no condition to launch a very serious attack.

In the end I found myself back at the hotel and had a coffee before going to bed.

Friday 16 October

Breakfast was very good and there seemed to be a wide choice. I only ate a bread roll and butter but there were lots of people eating eggs, sausage, ham, cheese and so on. I was surprised by how many Japanese there were around. One table had two Japanese men and two Poles. They talked partly in English but one of the Japanese also spoke what I think was Polish. It could have been Russian.

I waited downstairs for Magda. A girl walked up and down obviously waiting for someone but she was wearing a raincoat. Outside it was a bright fresh sunny morning.

When Madga came into the hotel lobby I recognized her immediately. She was wearing the jacket for a start but she was also the type I was expecting. She was casually dressed and somewhat windswept, but very

attractive and had a style that was familiar. She looked exactly as her equivalent in New York, London or Paris would look. This is a difference between Russia and Poland I think — nearly all the Russians we met — for instance the economics student on the train or Ivan's girl-friend looked Russian. The Poles I met simply looked European. I don't mean their cheekbones or eyes — I mean their style.

We shook hands and went to have coffee. Magda didn't want to have coffee in my hotel — she said it was 'nicer' in another place she knew.

Once more, as soon as we began talking, the seriousness and difficulty of life here started to become clearer — just as it had with Harry's friends the day before. She asked what I wanted to do or see and said she had all morning free. I said if it was not too deadly dull for her could we just walk about the streets and look at shops rather than seek out tourist attractions or beauty spots. She said OK. I said I wanted to go to a nearby travel agent to reserve a sleeper on my train.

As we walked along Magda became more and more interested in showing me things as she realized how little I knew and how fascinated I was in almost everything.

On the way to the travel agent, on one of Warsaw's main shopping streets, you immediately noticed the queues. I saw one about twenty-five to thirty yards long outside a completely empty butcher's shop. Mostly women were queuing, but there were boys and men there too. They chatted, read books or newspapers, and some just stood patiently in the sort of trance that queuing can put you in. Not only was the shop quite empty it was also closed. 'They are waiting in case there is a delivery of meat,' explained Magda. She said she had a maid, who was at that moment looking after her two-year-old child; having a maid was a great help, it meant she could work and go out and get on with life to a certain extent. But the maid had said when she accepted the job: 'I'll do anything — but I won't queue!'

In the travel agent's we had to wait for a few moments. While we waited Magda pointed out two Poles being attended to. 'You see, they are not travelling on passports,' she said. 'They have got what are called "travel documents". That means they are leaving the country — emigrating.' I looked and saw the documents. I asked if the staff minded dealing with people who were leaving. Magda shrugged: 'No, I don't think so — they are probably quite used to it.' She listened for a while and then smiled. 'He is going to West Germany. He was probably born in a part of Poland that was once German, and the Germans still recognize anyone born there as German.' She went on translating. 'The travel agent just asked "One way ticket?" "Yes." "You are leaving the country?" "Yes." "Then you want first travel to W ------ and just go." '
Magda said the man was being very kind and friendly to the client who didn't understand too readily what his route was.

Later we asked the travel agent how many people were leaving like this. He said about sixty a day through this office. And how long had this been going on?

'About two years at that rate. The recent troubles don't seem to have made much difference. It's just that since August 1980 the newspapers began to write about it.'

Back in the street Magda showed me a grocer and bread shop. There was a queue for bread, a heap of which was stacked at one end of the shop. At the other end all the shelves were empty except for some meat in a freezer. One or two women queued there. 'They are waiting for a delivery of meat too,' said Magda. The meat in the freezer was rabbit and they didn't want that. 'This used to be such a lovely shop,' she said looking round at the empty shelves. I looked at them too and found the sight disturbing. Alfred Hitchcock was famous in his films for making ordinary objects and everyday views sinister and threatening, and these silent, empty shelves had a Hitchcock-like quality of producing alarm and fear. They eloquently conveyed that somewhere nearby something dreadful had gone wrong.

'I want to show you something,' said Magda, hurrying me along the street. 'I have an American friend, she has dollars and can shop for me at the foreign goods shop.' This was a place where Poles, unless they were especially privileged, could not go and where as a rule all goods were plentiful. 'See.' said Magda. Inside one or two women were buying things. There were heaps of butter and cheeses and tinned food. A little meat — not much but a small choice. 'There's usually more,' said Magda with something like satisfaction in her voice. 'Things are even getting short here.'

There are many people in the West who believe that Communist states create equality whereas they openly create privileges on a scale that is barely conceivable in the West. In Communist states there are fat cats who can live well — not only way above the breadline but way above the law in many ways as it applies to their fellow-citizens.

Magda explained that she not only could sometimes get goods through her friends from this place but that she also had friends abroad who could send food parcels; and, if the winter got too rough, she could even fly away to friends in Paris or London until the spring. She said she was not exactly a passionate supporter of Solidarity, many of whose leaders she felt were on a bit of an ego trip, too keen on TV appearances and fame for her liking. As for the people from the Independent Poland Organization who were being tried for anti-state activity, she said their organization was tainted with anti-semitism and unpleasant nationalism. '. . . when people say "I am a *real* Pole" I don't like it.'

Every day something else becomes unavailable. She asked if I'd mind looking in an art material-cum-stationery shop for some notebooks. There were pitifully few goods on sale. When I realized what kind of books she was looking for I was able to tell her I had four that I had brought from Russia that she was very welcome to take, and I felt pleased to be of some use.

She said one effect of the shortages was that now you threw nothing away. She had recently dug out some old school noteboooks and used the unused pages and had mended a broken zipper because zips had vanished from the shops.

'Can't you just wire a friend in the West and say send some zips and notebooks?' I asked naively.

'Yes,' she said, 'once or twice perhaps for this or that — but not for everything everyday, and anyway you don't need a notebook sometime next week you need it *now*, so you make do.

'About a year ago,' she went on, 'I had got my life arranged exactly how I wanted it. I was married, I had a baby, a nice flat, I had changed my job from one paper to another that I preferred, and I felt I was set for a very productive and creative time of life, but now I spend my entire time just organizing life.

'Yesterday I queued for hours for petrol. I almost made it, but just before I got to the garage the petrol ran out. I went home so depressed and upset and angry I could scarcely bear it.' She paused. 'If I seemed a bit disorganized today it's because I haven't got over it yet.'

She told me another story. She had gone out looking for nappies for her little girl. She needed a supply because the family were going away for some time to a place where nappies were unavailable. She had found some in a shop and queued for a bit and had at last been told she could only buy two. She explained that she absolutely had to have more. The shopkeeper refused her. So she rejoined the queue and waited once more. When she again presented her request for two more nappies the man again refused. 'But I've queued again,' she protested. 'Makes no difference,' he said. At this point Magda's husband left the shop in a mixture of rage and embarrassment, but she stoutly argued for more nappies. At last another woman in the queue drew her aside and told her to wait. The next ten people in the queue after having bought what they wanted also purchased two nappies which they gave to Magda. The shopkeeper watched in a fury — but was unable to do anything about it except abuse Magda and say she should be ashamed of herself for hoarding.

(I was constantly looking for little present to take to my wife and children while I was away and in a shop during this walk with Magda I saw a little toy my youngest son might have liked. Magda was reluctant to go into the shop because it was here that the nappy incident had happened and she was not inclined to meet the shop man again. In the end we did go in but there was such a queue we left again.)

Several times during this morning walk Magda asked if I'd mind queuing with her for something or other. It was as if while she was being a marvellous and informative guide she was also hunting — alert for a shopping opportunity that was worth taking advantage of. Once she saw a queue for grapes at a stall on the pavement. She regarded it for a while saying that she just had to buy some, but decided to try to find some elsewhere with a shorter queue. Later she dived into a shop saying 'Ah! Here we are!' It was a greengrocer's shop and had a certain amount of vegetables, cabbages, carrots, onions, etc. on show. But the queue snaking round the shop was for the grapes that were stacked in boxes behind the counter. It took something like half-an-hour to buy the two kilos of grapes that Magda was allowed and I bought a kilo too. Two English women I told this little story to when I returned both said somewhat critically: 'Two kilos of grapes, what on earth did she need so much for?' as if to say the Poles' hardship was obviously somewhat exaggerated. A Polish girl in London said that, of course, anyone would queue for fruit especially for children; and she also understood, as the

English women didn't, that you automatically bought as much as you were allowed or could carry, to share with neighbours or friends who had not been lucky enough to find any.

We passed through the carefully reconstructed old city — every brick and stone built after the war to exactly reproduce the ancient market square and side streets. Surrounded as it is by new, ugly urban architecture I'm afraid for me my main reaction was one of sadness. The painstaking reproduction of what was once there serves more as a reminder of Nazi occupation than anything else. I had a similar sensation at Peter's Summer Palace in Leningrad.

I was shown a material store with row after row of empty shelves and one or two bolts of nylon or man-made fibre cloth lying unwanted on the counter. Two or three bored shop girls waited pointlessly, leaning, arms folded until closing time.

We stopped to have coffee in a little dark café which was full of people talking and smoking. Magda was exhausted with walking about and I felt guilty at dragging her round. She told me a story to illustrate how bad things were in Poland. The British Embassy had recently refused a visa to a singer friend of hers. The singer had been doing OK until the British officials had asked: 'What are your reasons for *coming back*?' She was unable to convince them that she wanted to return. I obviously expressed some amused disbelief at this tale because Magda said: 'You are smiling. I promise you it's true — she had no immediate family here — she is not married and they didn't believe her.'

On our way back to the hotel the queues still waited strung out along the pavement in the early afternoon sun. There was no sense of a lunch-break or rush hour in the streets, by the way. Magda told me people tended to eat or take breaks at odd times during the day. Each time I had lunch with Poles in Warsaw we sat down to eat at 3.00, 3.30 p.m. or even later. I liked the arrangment very much.

The presents I had been given in London to distribute or pass on in Warsaw, I had divided up into five piles, because I had been given five addresses. But I was uncertain whether I had given the appropriate goodies to each family. I asked Magda to come up to my room to simply choose what she wanted. She swapped tea for instant coffee and soap for dried fruit. I cursed inwardly that I had not brought more — how pathetic a little heap it looked now and how big and heavy when I was packing in London.

I added a tin of herrings from the fridge and carried the stuff home for Magda. She lived only fifteen minutes walk or less from the hotel. She said she'd ring later. She and her husband were going to take me to two parties in the evening if they could get some petrol.

I tried to say, without seeming ungrateful or unenthusiastic, that I

107

hoped they were going anyway and this was not something they felt they had to lay on for me. 'I want to go,' she said. 'I'm not sure about Roman.' I felt uncomfortable but she laughed and said she'd ring later.

All the Russians I had met in the USSR with the possible exception of Ivan had left me feeling in one sense superior. They made me feel western and therefore sophisticated and worldly in a way they could not be. After all, I had travelled and read and talked in ways that were impossible for them — but this was emphatically not true of the Poles. From the first to the last they all gave me the opposite feeling if anything. They too had travelled and read and certainly talked — and they had also fought and tangled with a system that gave them some of the charisma that veterans always have and they left me feeling inexperienced and overprotected. Magda had studied in London, lived in London, lived in Paris and California and holidayed in the South of France. I realized as I had never realized before what the Russian occupation of Eastern Europe meant — I felt suddenly as angry as I might if I heard Russians had taken over Paris or London. A ridiculous phrase began to go round and round my head: 'I've seen the future — and it hurts.' Another phone call came in the afternoon. A friend of Ryczard, who was also on my list, rang to say he would like to take me out and show me round tomorrow, and give me lunch *and* dinner in the evening to meet a few friends. I was overwhelmed by the friendliness and generosity with which he proposed all this and arranged to meet him at 11.00 a.m. the next morning.

In the evening Magda and Roman rang to say they were waiting downstairs and we were going to the parties. . . .

Roman drove faster than I've ever been driven in a city before. Tyres screaming, he tore round corners and headed for intersections with suicidal confidence. Mercifully there was very little traffic but I was really frightened and hung on as I was thrown violently about in the back of the little car. I wondered if Roman always drove like this or whether it was his way of protesting about having to go out, or maybe a general expression of rage against everything. I wanted to shout at him: 'Listen, you fucking idiot, you've got no petrol — your tank is reading empty — if you drove slowly what petrol you have got would take you twice as far. . . .' But in fact I watched in horrified silence as the needle on his speedo hovered around 180 km/h.

We screeched to a stop outside some flats. Magda, who obviously considered this a perfectly usual speed at which to progress through the city, explained that this was where her parents lived and that they had agreed to give some petrol. One can appeared and was fed into the car. It had contained so little petrol that the indicator still read empty. More was produced and after ten minutes or so we shot off out into a hideous suburb of new high-rise blocks in, as far as I could tell, unmarked roads. We got lost. Magda and Roman shouted at each other. Every time Roman went to turn right Magda would shout: 'Left! Left!' Roman would say: 'You are crazy,' but he would turn left. After a tense few minutes Magda would begin to bounce in her seat: 'I was right! I was right.' 'She is always right,' said Roman with an odd Polish mixture of bad temper and pride.

Out of a nightmare forest of brand new, indeed unfinished, high-rise blocks they eventually chose one. I couldn't tell how they did it. We picked our way over a muddy forecourt or open space which was littered with rubble, heaps of scaffolding and cement mixers.

'What do you think of it?' asked Roman. 'I think it is frightening,' I said as I looked at the barren ugliness that stretched in every direction.

Roman misunderstood what I meant. 'You are right,' he said waving a bottle of vodka. 'This place is full of gangsters who would gladly attack you to get this.'

The flat was brand new and barely furnished. As far as I could tell it was a house-warming party. The people were all young — late twenties — and casually dressed exactly as similar types in England would be. Jeans, jerseys, beards, and so on. It was a very good-looking crowd and there was a cheerful and friendly atmosphere.

I discovered that most of them spoke incredibly good English — several worked as translators and the men I spoke to had all travelled widely in the West. Working as a translator (of novels) could be a bit frustrating. There was enormous demand for translations of modern novels — it would be possible to sell hundreds of thousands of copies — but there was no paper to print them on, and months and months of work could more or less go for nothing as publishing dates were put off due to shortages.

I was given a shot of vodka, which I drained instantly to try to help myself relax a little, and was instantly handed a glass of champagne. I noticed Roman draining his glass too and my heart sank at the thought of the return journey. But then I noticed Magda refusing drinks and realized she was going to drive home. I learned that drunken driving, or even driving after one drink even though you had not been involved in an accident, might be severely punished. (The same was true in Russia. At lunch with Ivan I noticed he did not touch his wine for this reason.)

We were given curry and rice to eat. There was plenty of it and it was very good. I chatted to an American. A musician who was married to a Polish girl and had lived here for several years. In many ways life had been good for him here. He travelled around all over East and West Europe teaching and playing. His life was much more varied and full of possibility than it would have been at home in the States. But the

109

political situation was getting him down a bit and I gathered he was going to leave soon.

This very highly educated middle-class crowd plunked down in what at home would be a poor, working-class apartment, took some getting used to. I mean, I wouldn't get used to it. To my western trained eyes it just looked strange.

After an hour or so Magda and Roman announced we were leaving and we rushed out. I wondered if Roman felt he was rather grand; there was something about the way we dropped in and left while the party was obviously just beginning that smacked of putting in an appearance.

The next party was weird. It was in a large old house, not a flat, and was full of arty people. Magda explained there were famous actors and writers here. Dissidents and intellectuals and so on. And they looked it. The atmosphere was again very middle-class but what gave the evening its weirdness was the house — or rather its contents. Its owner collected naive Polish art. Religious, erotic, peasant, urban, old or new, and every tiny little bit of space was occupied by a painting or a carving or an object of some sort. On the stairs, on countless shelves, on the ceiling, under the carpets, in cupboards, on the banisters, suspended, balanced, piled simply everywhere. Magda and I wandered round and I looked. Some of the stuff was junk but much of it was wonderful. Several sculptures and carvings and some curious objects, half carving half painting, like three-dimensional pictures, I thought were terrific. The effect of the whole house was one of absolute madness. You would have to be crazy to actually live there — and if you weren't you soon would be.

I didn't talk to anyone and I wasn't introduced to anyone. Magda asked if I wanted to be but I said: 'No, I don't know what to say to them.' 'Neither do I,' she said.

I was glad to go home to the hotel. I was exhausted; even Magda and Roman had stopped yelling at each other. I guess they were tired too. When I said goodnight I also said I'd telephone again before I left. I did call once or twice but I either got no answer or spoke to a woman, presumably the maid, who could not understand what I said.

Saturday 17 October

At 10.00 am I was waiting in the lobby with Wojtek. As usual there were a number of people waiting and chatting there. I saw a man come in in jogging clothes, and a girl in a long stylish raincoat, high-heeled boots and smart shoulder bag was pacing up and down. Several groups of Japanese hung about and some Americans. The general scene was brighter and jollier than a similar one in Russia. But not nearly so lively as the equivalent lobby in the USA.

One day earlier this year in New York I was with my family on Fifth Avenue near the Metropolitan Museum of Art. Roller-skating backwards down the Avenue was a tall young Black man. He was travelling fast and moving gracefully and he was wearing brilliant coloured clothes and a striped scarf. Under his arm he carried some books or papers and he had headphones over his ears wired to a miniature tape deck in his breast pocket. In a moment he swirled out of sight and was gone but he remained in my mind's eye a beautiful image of American individuality. No one took much notice of him, the cars steered round him — he wasn't harming anyone, he was having a great time. I don't think such a sight would ever be seen anywhere in the Soviet Union, and probably not in Warsaw. But the point I think I'm labouring to make is that the hotel lobby I was waiting in was a step nearer that New York scene than anything I saw in Moscow or Leningrad, even though it had a way to go. There was at least a jogger in a track suit and some chic girls.

When Wojtek arrived, tall and bearded, we recognized each other immediately. He said he had his two small daughters in his car outside and proposed to drive me round Warsaw to show me sights and to walk a bit any time we felt like it. This sounded a perfect arrangement but I felt extremely awkward about him using up his precious petrol in this way.

'Look,' he said. 'If I choose to use my petrol this way it means I will have a petrol crisis on Tuesday instead of Wednesday — what's the difference?' he smiled reassuringly.

His well-behaved children, aged eleven and nine, spoke no English. They shook hands politely.

Saturday morning in Warsaw was slightly different to Friday. There were not so many shoppers in the streets and more strollers; groups of tourists (Polish and East Germans I gathered), weekenders looking at the old city and relaxing. There were a few queues and very few cars.

We drove to Wilanáw, the beautiful palace and gardens on the outskirts of the city. Enclosed by the trees and enjoying the sunshine on the leafy paths you got a sense of what this city must once have been; and the jangling effect of the clashing styles in the rebuilt centre gave way to the peaceful pleasures of seventeenth-century architecture and gardens.

As we talked our conversation was entirely concerned with politics, Solidarity and the gigantic problems facing the country. I began to get the idea that, at the heart of the matter, there were simply two Polands. There was the Government's Poland which the party was continuing to run and there was Solidarity's Poland which, though young and very inexperienced, was very big and very ambitious and very, very powerful. These two opposed Polands looked with contemptuous and angry hostility at each other while desperately trying to do, by their lights, the

111

best for the country. The only thing was that Solidarity has got so big and its momentum was so swift that the unwieldy and discredited party could do little but look on in horror as Solidarity ignored the party line.

For instance, there were underground papers which flatly contradict the information given in the official papers. Everyone knew that the official Press was garbage, and believed the underground information. Wojtek also said people were far less careful of talking on the phone. They knew it was bugged but they were getting into the habit of talking frankly.

There was nothing dashing or melodramatic or romantic about Wojtek's attitude to the mighty changes that had happened in this country. He described himself as a Solidarity activist and had a serious, thoughtful and I thought patient approach to the future. All one felt of a more exciting element in his manner was below the surface: an absolutely rock hard certainty that he and his colleagues were on the right track and there was no going back. His concern for the future had apparently no fear in it — or if he was afraid he was not deterred.

After walking round the palace he led me through the gardens to a little museum where there was an exhibition of posters and pictures he wanted us to see.

When we got there it was closed. He frowned in exasperation and muttered something to himself. Then he smiled and turning he said: 'Before I came here this morning I looked in the paper and I checked by phone that this was open — it proves what I was saying just now — you cannot believe ANYTHING in the official press.'

We drove back into town and he parked across the road from the building — once a school — where Solidarity now had its headquarters. Over the main doors hung a banner demanding or proclaiming a free trade union movement. Outside the building there were several concrete notice boards plastered with posters.

Wojtek said: 'It is extraordinary for us to see posters like this openly displayed in our country.' He translated the defiant and bold slogans and messages on the posters. One showed a pretty toddler in a green field wearing a Solidarity sash with the legend 'one year old'. Wojtek told me this poster had appeared altered by official party critics of Solidarity; a box of matches had been placed in the baby's hand and the slogan read: 'Don't play with fire'.

Inside the building there was considerable bustle with people constantly entering and leaving and a light buzz of conversation came down the corridor and the clatter and thump of footsteps. 'Usually it's much busier than this,' said Wojtek.

To our left stretched a corridor and in the corridor, stacked five or six feet high in places, was a heap of foolscap-sized packets of typing-paper.

Reception desk at Solidarity headquarters - Warsaw Oct 1981

It was on this paper, Wojtek explained, that Solidarity's newspaper was printed. New supplies came in every day, brought by citizens who had found paper for sale somewhere in the city. 'They buy it, bring it here and add it to the pile,' said Wojtek. It was a very touching sight.

Paper was very short and distribution of newspapers was also difficult to organize so newspapers were circulated once a week, but news was also telexed round the country to Solidarity centres every day and published on noticeboards and news sheets locally. There was an exhibition of photographs down the other side of the corridor. There were photographs of meetings and orators and so on. One lot of photographs particularly excited Wojtek.

'This', he said, 'is the most extraordinary story of all.' The photographs were of a preliminary court hearing at which a Solidarity man was suing a Communist trade union leader called Albin Siwak. Siwak in the course of a prolonged attack had tired of heaping the usual sort of abuse on the Solidarity's man's head and began calling him a bigamist and thief and generally attacking him in a more personal way. As far as I could gather the Solidarity man had let Siwak run on for a few days and had then appealed to a court, demanding protection from these scandalous lies, and the court had no alternative but to do what he demanded and the first hearing had been held. Siwak had been ordered to appear before the court but had not done so, explaining that he had not got the message in time, or some such idiotic excuse. To Wojtek this hearing was of enormous importance and its outcome crucial. 'You probably cannot understand,' he said. 'But it is simply unheard of for a Communist leader to have to answer in this way for his actions. It just doesn't happen.' Once again I got the feeling of Solidarity sweeping the Communist party onwards — and that weedy little hacks such as Siwak were finding to their amazement that they were being pushed aside by a tide they could not turn. Wojtek was not nearly so cool relating this story to me — on the contrary he was obviously elated by it.

He asked if I would like to meet any Solidarity officials to ask them questions — to interview them. I was very torn by wishing to take advantage of this offer and knowing that I didn't really know how. I was not well enough up on the situation to exploit it properly and so I said 'no' — I'd rather just talk to him. I tried to explain my reasons and he shrugged and said 'as you like'. (I had often been interviewed myself by people who knew absolutely nothing about cartoons or drawing or other artists and it was a very irritating experience — I did not want to risk irritating a Solidarity official in the same way.) I wanted to buy some posters and badges but the little shop was closed. Wojtek said I should come back on Monday morning and it would be open.

We drove to Wojtek's apartment. On the way we passed a queue of cars waiting for petrol. The queue was about a kilometre long, Wojtek estimated. It stretched away down the street from the garage and wound its way round a housing estate. People drove their cars to the queue and left them there — sometimes for twenty-four hours — returning now and then during the day to move them up as the queue had shifted forward during their absence. There were quite wide gaps in the queue where empty cars had not yet been moved. No one apparently tried to sneak into these places. Little knots of patient drivers chatted on the roadside; here and there someone read a book or paper; some simply sat waiting. The garage at the head of the queue was closed. 'There may be a delivery later,' said Wojtek. He half smiled, half winced at the idea of the terrible wait his fellow-citizens were in for. He lived in a block among many other blocks and I couldn't help being aware of a certain falling of my spirits as we drove deeper and deeper into the housing estate. It was so ugly and boring and depressing. I felt a sort of relief when Wojtek's daughters said hello to some children as we walked from the car; it made one realize life went on even in this dump. The apartment itself was light and simply furnished — I immediately noticed books and paintings and a shelf of records. It was not large, not very comfortable, but nothing like as depressing once you were in it as you thought it was going to be when you approached.

Wojtek's wife Krystyna was out at a film and was coming back later. He prepared lunch and we drank some wine. The children disappeared into their room and played quietly.

Wojtek pointed to a half-finished building a few yards away across a bit of open ground. It was a new school. When these flats were built the builders had a 'plan'. So many dwellings had to be produced by a certain time. No mention was made of shops, playgrounds, or schools and consequently none were provided because to do so would make it impossible, or much more difficult, to fulfil the plan. The only school was about a kilometre away and became so crowded that the children were taught in shifts, some getting to school at 8.00 in the morning and waiting until 4.00 in the afternoon before getting any tuition. 'They even did gymnastics on the STAIRS!' said Wojtek. The teachers eventually threatened to strike, not for more money or better conditions for themselves, but they said they would no longer tolerate seeing the children 'educated' in this appalling way. The support for the teachers was so overwhelming, their argument and demands so watertight and reasonable, that a new school was instantly planned and begun.

'We have lost a bit more open ground,' said Wojtek, pointing out a few surviving vegetable patches and flower beds, 'but it was necessary.'

For lunch we had chicken, potatoes and salad, with chocolate for pudding. I felt ridiculously awkward eating it. I felt I should not take food that had probably taken ages to buy, and were I not there, would provide at least part of another meal. But it would have been even more awkward to refuse it.

Later in the afternoon Krystyna, Wojtek's wife, returned. She also spoke English, not quite as well as Wojtek. She was a librarian and had been watching the latest film being shown in a festival given to the work of Sidney Lumet (the director of *Serpico* and *Dog Day Afternoon*). She had been disappointed by the film. She wore a large Solidarity badge pinned on her jersey. Krystyna had been in London and had loved going to pubs. She tried to remember the name of one somewhere in the West End she had particularly liked. In the company of this charming and intelligent family I was struck once more by the fact that the Russians were Russians and however grisly their political system, they had devised it themselves and its origins lay in their own tormented history. But the Poles were an occupied nation. The Russian system under which Poland suffered was just as much an affront as it would be in Britain or France — and I was aware of a depressed kind of rage growing in myself on their behalf.

Krystyna and Wojtek took me for a walk in a park, using up more precious petrol. The children did not accompany us. 'They are so lazy,' complained Wojtek.

'What will they do while we are out?' I asked. 'Watch TV suppose.'

'No,' said Wojtek. 'They have been forbidden to watch TV for a week as a punishment because they were naughty.'

I smiled at hearing this familiar punishment being used in Poland and said it was a threat we constantly used against our children too but it was very difficult to enforce. Wojtek shrugged and I got the feeling he and Krystyna had more control over their kids than I had over mine. The park was very pretty in the autumn afternoon. I was delighted by the palace by the lake and horrified by the Chopin Memorial — a great ugly thing.

In the evening Krystyna prepared for the dinner party that she had organized. I opened tins of fish for her and cut up bread while she made salads and cooked a pasta dish. She played records by Johnny Cash and sang along in perfect Western cowboy English. Most of their large collection of records were of classical music but there was some jazz and folk music. Johnny Cash seemed a most unlikely singer in this east European setting — but Krystyna obviously loved him.

We started eating dinner in a desultory kind of way at about 9.00. The children were still playing around and Krystyna said: 'Eat, go on, help yourself — I don't know when or if my guests are arriving.' I could not make out whether this doubt was just normal or whether it was caused by the petrol shortage.

Enormous shots of vodka were poured out and almost immediately I began to feel tipsy. I was also terribly tired and aware of the strain of constantly talking to people who did not speak very good English. In such a circumstance the expression of the simplest notion can involve a great effort to find easily understood vocabulary or grammar. You begin to act like an idiot who cannot communicate or talk to intelligent people as if they were idiots who cannot understand. It is exhausting.

By about 10.00 the other guests had arrived; Ryczard and Ania; a doctor and her husband, who I think worked with computers; and a film writer. All spoke English, some better than others — though most of the conversation was in Polish.

This whole evening was most difficult. The guests were all close friends of my Polish acquaintance in London. These days they very rarely met and my presence was the excuse for their little party. But although I had in a way brought them together, there was very little I could say to them, or bring to the evening other than my simple and somewhat awkward presence. As soon as they had drunk a little vodka and eaten some food a strange giggly mood gripped them. Krystyna began it. In the middle of a conversation with the doctor she began laughing and was soon helpless. She put a hanky in her mouth to try to stop and waved her hand at the doctor to say 'be quiet' but still she shook with laughter and tears poured down her cheeks. Soon Ryczard too was laughing and giggling with her and Ania actually got up and staggered from the room holding her side and covering her eyes, speechless with wild amusement. In the theatre getting the giggles like this is called 'corpsing' and soon they were all corpsing and quite unable to stop. Now and then one of them, touched by my puzzled and embarrassed expression, attempted to explain the 'joke'.

'You see,' he said. 'The word tooth — which in Polish also means — oh what is it — how do you say it — you see when you, in Poland, say the word which is hole — no gap . . . ' These efforts shed very little light on the joke and reduced the party to absolutely unashamed hysteria. They would take one look at the struggling translator, another at my glassy smile and nearly choke with laughter — gasping, waving their hands, giving up all attempts to restrain themselves. Now and then, as happens during such storms, a pregnant silence fell and they would all look at their plates wondering what to say next. The doctor would then intone in English 'Our situation is very serious', and before she'd finished they would be off again.

The film writer said at some time during the evening: 'I queued for an hour today and got my petrol — and I found a watch.'

'It was your lucky day,' said Wojtek.

'Not really — it was a Russian watch,' said the writer with a chuckle.

Later, driving home with Ryczard and Ania, Ania apologized to me saying: 'I hope you were not offended — you understand we are all old friends and we very rarely meet . . . also the tension and anxiety we all feel these days produces these silly jokes and fits of giggles — it's a way of letting off steam.' I understood only too well, and had not been offended — my embarrassment was more to do with feeling like a voyeur, a westerner on a sort of slumming trip to the East. There was much more to it than just not understanding their language that made me feel an outsider.

Wojtek had told me earlier that the doctor was not practising at the moment partly because she had a young child but also because being a doctor when certain drugs and equipment were in such short supply was very depressing; also too many of her patients were coming to her and in effect asking her to cure them of the stress caused by shortages and queues and uncertainty. She had said to Wojtek: 'I cannot help them — I am not a psychiatrist.' The doctor was a thin, fierce-looking young woman with a piece of sticking plaster over one eye, which gave her a vaguely piratical look. She was the only one of them who smoked. She made me feel nervous. Before I left she approached me and said, I thought in a rather sarcastic way: 'I think I like you after all.' I didn't reply. I was not sure whether I had offended her somehow and was being forgiven or whether, being a bit deaf, I had heard wrong, or whether her bad English had not been up to saying what she really meant. I couldn't make sense of the remark.

One way and another I did not feel I had risen to the evening. I wished Harry had been there to sing for my supper, or that I had swotted up on Poland a hell of a lot more before going there.

Sunday 18 October

At breakfast the next morning I sat at the counter because all the tables were taken by a huge party. I waited some time before I was served. A woman sat a couple of places down also waiting and grew impatient. A large middle-aged man with a red face said: 'Excuse me, sir,' in a strange accent and I moved my bag from the seat next to me to allow him to sit. Almost immediately he began saying in a loud voice in English: 'This is Solidarity for you, you know — it's disgraceful — that is why we are waiting — it's Solidarity. . . . All talk they are and no action . . . They are probably out there having a meeting.' I looked at him, and was about to ask him was he Polish when a waitress appeared and put down a menu in front of me and one in front of the man. Instead of looking at it he stood up and said: 'It's too late now,' and muttering furiously about Solidarity he walked out. The waitress looked surprised then pulled a

118

little face, shrugged and took my order and that of the woman sitting nearby. The latter asked me what all that was about, and we fell into conversation. She was an American correspondent called Sonya and had been in Poland for some time. She asked me what I was doing here. I told her and recounted some of the conversations I'd had with Poles. She was particularly interested in the building of the new school and the story of the depressed doctor. I would have liked to have given her the phone numbers I had so that she could have written up these tales and, no doubt, find others, but I couldn't for fear of intensely irritating my new Polish friends. I said I'd try to find out whether they would consider talking to her.

After breakfast I met Ryczard in the lobby. To my relief the first thing he said was that he had no car. 'I could not get petrol,' he said. 'We must go by bus.'

Outside it was raining quite hard and in the centre of the wide square in front of the hotel a crowd was gathering — sheltering under umbrellas. Ryczard told me they were waiting to see the ceremonial changing of the guard at the tomb of the unknown soldier who rests beneath an eternal flame nearby. 'Would you like to see it?'

I was getting into the habit of saying 'Yes' to everything; it made life easier in some ways and was more likely to lead to rewarding and unexpected experiences. I didn't really want to stand in the rain to watch a lot of soldiers getting wet but I said 'Yes', and to my surprise Ryczard said: 'Good — I've never seen it before!' He had seen the changing of the guard at Buckingham Palace. 'I never have,' I admitted.

The ceremony was simple and like all such rituals. The goose-stepping was less Nazi-like than the Red Square lot changing guard on the Lenin 'doll'. The officers looked proud and the troops looked wet. There was quite a bit of military music. The exciting sound of officers' distant voices shouting orders above the din and the crash of boots slamming to attention was spoiled by the fact that a civilian with a raincoat on his head carried a microphone round and held it in front of the man giving commands, so the whole thing was broadcast very loud.

I glanced at Ryczard and saw he was watching the military display grinning like a schoolboy. He was very tall and was wearing a beret like a Frenchman. He saw me look at him and his smile broadened and he raised his eyebrows in mock excitement.

I couldn't help wondering if the ridiculously youthful-looking soldiers wouldn't soon be engaged in some less harmless and safe duties, either facing enraged and suffering Poles or regiments of Russians.

Ryczard suggested we visit the Art Gallery and we caught a bus. In Warsaw citizens carry round little books of bus tickets that they buy from kiosks and tear them off and punch them on little machines inside

their buses, trolleys or trams. All this transport, Ryczard said, was
breaking down. No spare parts and very bad maintenance was leading to
a transport crisis. The buses were bought from France some years ago
and now everyone said they were a terrible buy: apart from the fact that
they were already worn out they gave an exceptionally jolting and rough
ride and reeked, inside and out, of diesel fumes. Ryczard said there
would literally be no public transport in Warsaw in six months' time.

We descended from the bus near the Communist Party headquarters.
'The White House' Ryczard called it sardonically. I had understood
Wojtek the day before to call the Soviet Embassy 'The White House' and
he'd also called the Soviet Trade Centre 'The Little White House'.
Maybe they call every state building a White House.

Ryczard nodded at the building and said: 'They are working away like
mad in there — but they don't know what to do.' He grinned.

Inside the gallery there was an enormous queue of people waiting to
leave their coats. It was compulsory to leave coats or at least it seemed to
be when it was raining. But there were no security checks on bags either
here or in the USSR. The queue was moving very slowly because there
was no room to hang more coats — new ones were taken in only when
others were taken out. One woman was dealing with this poorly arranged
system. The queue was incredibly patient and well behaved. People
seemed to settle down to queue as we might settle down for coffee. I said
I'd like to look at the postcards or try to buy a catalogue of an exhibition
of Picasso etchings that was being held here. This involved another
queue. There were no catalogues — sold out and almost no postcards.
What there was for sale was on show behind glass inside a little cubicle
where a salesgirl sat. Because of the queue you couldn't look into the
cubicle until it was your turn to buy something, so without holding
everyone up while you asked to look at things shopping was difficult.
You really had to know what you wanted before you queued. Browsing
was out.

The Picassos depressed me. They were late etchings and nearly all
were of young girls displaying their twats to desperate-looking gnome-
like old men. Upstairs we walked through galleries of huge paintings of
heroic scenes from Poland's bloody past. Now and then a painter stood
out. I wrote down the names of three. I've now lost the bit of paper and
can only remember Michaelowich — whose bold portraits and paintings
of horses were outstanding. There was an interesting mad painter of the
late nineteenth century, a sort of Polish Dadd. I remember a double
portrait of two girls who stood unaware of a lion-sized dragonfly
hovering overhead, and there was one other early twentieth-century
painter I liked whose best work was a picture of a row of dolls.

Several galleries were closed off and it was hard to see why. Ryczard asked an attendant who said the heating was not on in those galleries and it was too cold for the attendants to sit in them. The pictures could not be left unattended. Actually this seemed silly to me because warm air from the other rooms was circulating freely, but there it was. I wondered vaguely about keeping valuable paintings in rooms where the temperature varied in this way.

Ryczard, who was one of the most perfectly mannered people I've ever met, said what a pleasure it was to have an excuse for visiting the art gallery. He said it was years since he'd been here and these days what with the shortages and Solidarity meetings and general difficulties it was too rare to do such things as look at paintings, have outings or read. All one's energy was taken up just surviving.

We walked from the gallery to his apartment. He lived in a block built just after the war. The flats were intended for high-up party officials and were large, solid and spacious. He owned one half of a divided flat on the ground floor, and was busy doing some conversions to make separate rooms for his children. He also hoped to buy the other half of the flat when the present occupiers moved out. They were an old couple. The state was keen to sell property of this kind in order to make money to build more housing. Ania was cooking lunch and putting the baby down for its afternoon rest. Ania's young sister, aged about twenty-two, was playing with an older child, a little girl of about two years. Ania's sister spoke very good French; she had lived in Paris as an *au pair* I think, to learn the language.

The meal was delicious and there was plenty of it. Meat in a sort of stew — with bulghur and then salad. For pudding there was jelly which was served with a carton of what looked like cream. I asked what it was. 'Not cream,' said Ania, as if to say: 'I'm sorry, but where would we get such a luxury.' 'It's cheese.' Actually it tasted rather like a sort of very mild sour cream. I liked it.

I was surprised how strict Ryczard was with his little daughter. Several times he spoke quite sharply to her when she dropped a dollop of food down her front — or squidged up some food with her fingers. She didn't seem to mind being ticked off and obediently stopped what she was told to stop. Memories of my children spraying food around the kitchen at the same age made me feel quite ashamed of my soft indulgence.

After lunch another of Ania's sisters arrived. She was an older woman and came accompanied by her two tall teenage sons and her husband. She had just returned, by boat, from spending a fortnight apple-picking in Sweden. Her husband had driven all the way to the coast to pick her up. I was puzzled as to why and how he could do that during such a serious petrol shortage. Why hadn't she come by train? The reason was that she had come back heavily laden with all kinds of goods that were unobtainable in Poland and that it would have been impossible for her to carry on the train. Her husband had filled his trunk and then every available can he could get his hands on and with his little car like a petrol bomb on wheels had managed to make the journey without stopping at a garage. 'It was like the olden days,' he said, 'driving through the country without another car on the road.' He made it sound like fun, as if it had all been worth it for the drive alone.

This family stayed for tea and before they left said they'd heard a rumour that Kania, the president, had been removed from office. This news interested them all of course but they seemed to take it extraordinarily calmly and, having resolved to listen to the news at 5.00, went on chatting and laughing about family and personal matters.

I watched Ryczard kissing his sister-in-law's hand as he said goodbye. I wished I knew how to do that gracefully. It was the most attractive sight. Poles kiss women's hands all the time — I always enjoyed watching this courtly and old-fashioned gesture.

By 5.00 both children were up and about. The girl sat on Ryczard's knee as he bent listening intently to the news on the radio. He shushed her gently as she chatted away and tried to distract his attention. Ania spoonfed the baby and mainly concentrated on that happy task while she gave me a running translation of what the news-reader was saying.

They learnt of Kania's removal and the appointment of Jaruzelski with little reaction. 'What does it mean?' I asked. 'We cannot tell what it means,' said Ryczard. 'It is impossible to tell whether this is good or bad news. The change is meaningless. They all come from the same root.'

'What are they saying now?' I asked later. 'It's a kind of appeal or resolution from the Government,' explained Ania. Ryczard was making contemptuous little spluttering noises now and again. 'It's an attack on Solidarity. They are saying there must be a return to normality and end to strikes and so on.'

Ryczard said: 'They do not have the backing of the people. It's just the same old stuff.' He smiled. 'We've heard it all before.'

'Isn't it frightening?' I asked. 'Aren't you alarmed to hear your movement attacked like that?'

'No,' he said. 'They've done it so often before. I am still optimistic.'

It was impossible not to be impressed by the firm and calm resolution in his voice and manner. If I had been a Government spy I would have thought that short of shooting him it was going to be bloody difficult to stop him from going right on with his Solidarity work.

Ania continued to feed the baby, grimacing and smiling as the child dribbled and ate.

I played with the toddler, trying to make him walk his first step while

Ania quickly dashed off a letter to her friend in London for me to carry home. Then I said goodbye and Ryczard escorted me to the bus stop. I said I could find my own way but he insisted on walking with me through the dark rainy streets. He explained that he was going out anyway, to church.

Back at the hotel when I got out of the lift and began walking to my room a curious incident occurred. Walking towards me down the otherwise deserted corridor came two young men. They were somewhat roughly dressed in jeans and windcheaters and were walking one behind the other in an odd kind of formation. I was instantly alarmed by something about them. I hesitated a moment and then walked rather warily towards them. They were both staring at me fixedly and I thought 'Christ! They are going to attack me.' One swerved towards me and I instantly sidestepped out of his way, my fists doubled and suddenly I flushed with anger and fear. At the same moment the other boy called something out and we passed by one another without anything happening. I did not look round until I had turned a corner and arrived at my door. There, instead of going in I waited, looking back the way I'd come. After a moment one of them looked round the corner and immediately he saw me disappeared again. I continued to wait and this happened again. After a bit I walked back down the corridor to the corner, very curious and now more angry than afraid. They had vanished and I didn't see them again.

Once in my room I felt alarmed again. The hotel was so huge and quiet and these menacing figures ranging the great empty corridors were extraordinarily sinister.

I telephoned home, glad I was leaving the next day.

I didn't leave the hotel again but had dinner in the restaurant. There I met the American journalist Sonya, also having a solitary dinner. I sat down at her invitation, very pleased to be able to talk English with an English speaker.

I told her that I had got the impression that my Polish friends were not that keen to be interviewed and she said OK she quite understood. I told her about the two marauders upstairs and she said that she had frequently felt very nervous in the hotel when returning to her room — and often had not opened her room door until some man walking nearby had moved away. 'That's when you're most vulnerable — just as you open your door. They push you in and . . .' She pulled a face. She told me that a colleague of hers had been taking a bath in his room the other day and had thought he heard his door open. He got up to investigate and found a young man going through the pockets of his clothes. The thief fled with a wallet. She told me how to lock my door — there was a way I had not noticed.

123

We found we had mutual acquaintances and I really enjoyed talking — it was such a relief not to feel retarded.

Monday 19 October

My last day in Warsaw. The first thing I did was to discover that I could get my transit visa to cross East Germany on the train. The young man in the travel office I went to had told me to be absolutely sure my papers were in order before I had anything to do with the East Germans. His hatred for them was quite surprising.

'Listen,' he said. 'Those East Germans are not kidding. In my opinion,' he continued, 'they are simply Fascists. They have arrived at being Fascists by a roundabout route.' His hands described a circle in the air. 'Make sure your visa is OK.'

I was a little worried about the East Germans. Sonya had told me that the last time she had taken a train ride across to West Germany the East German guards had confiscated all her Solidarity material, including badges, posters and newspapers — and also notebooks and other material from her bags. I began to be worried about my notebooks again.

I checked all my things into a left luggage place in the hotel and paid my bill to be ready for a quick getaway to catch my train in the afternoon.

There were two things I wanted to do before I left. The first was to return to the Solidarity headquarters to buy badges and posters. I walked, finding my way quite easily with my map. It was fine weather again and the queues were as long and tedious-looking as ever. I thought that it was not going to be so pleasant in the dead of winter to wait for two or three hours on these pavements.

Outside the Solidarity building I glanced at the posters Wojtek had showed me two days before. Every single one had been torn and ripped down.

There was considerably more activity inside the building than there had been at the weekend, and I sat waiting for the little shop to open and sketched two workers manning a reception desk.

A girl was also waiting and we chatted. She spoke almost perfect English. She was doing a course in 'tourism' and knew English and German. She had visited where she had relatives. When the little shop opened we stood together as a young man spread out the things that were for sale on the little counter. He put down a pile of books by Milosz.

'Do you see those books?' said the girl. 'Milosz. They are banned.' A young man picked one up casually and began reading it.

I bought my badges and failed to get any posters. 'Sold out,' said the girl. The shop boy began looking for change. 'Forget,' I said. He stopped looking for change and looked up to the next person in the queue.

I had one last thing I wanted to do. Sonya had told me that a synagogue had just opened in Warsaw. She had shown me where it was on my map and I wanted to go and look at it — perhaps visit it even. I set off and soon found the street. Nearby was a large Catholic Church and I looked inside. It was spotlessly clean and decorated here and there with flowers. Several people were moving about or sitting inside and the place looked like a healthy going concern. A large coloured photograph of the Pope caught my eye.

Back in the street I searched for the synagogue. But I couldn't find it. To and fro down the street I went. I either had the wrong address or it was so small — Sonya had said it was on the first floor of an old building — that I couldn't see it. I looked into a yard and an old lady said something to me.

I said: 'I'm looking for the synagogue.' She laughed, spread her hands and replied in Polish. I shrugged. She spoke a few words of German. I replied in French. 'Nein,' she said chuckling. 'Nein.' It was getting late and I walked back to the hotel. On the way I passed a wide doorway leading to a yard. It looked very ancient. The road there was cobbled. It was clearly a fragment of Warsaw the Nazis had not destroyed. Two battered metal lions crouched each side of the doorway — acting as bollards to prevent vehicles hitting the walls. It was like finding evidence of a lost civilization in a wilderness.

I had lunch at the hotel — trout and vegetables and a glass of beer. I was so anxious to be on my way home that I got up and paced about telling myself not to get to the station too ridiculously early. There was over an hour to go. I remembered Harry finding at the last minute his train went from a different station and asked at the travel desk would they check my station. The man looked at a timetable and couldn't find my train. 'Perhaps it's out of date,' he said. I knew which station was mine anyway and told him not to worry.

To kill time I strolled in a park and at last permitted myself to get my bags and coat and find a taxi. There were several taxis waiting but the doorman practically forced me into a car waiting at the curb that was not a taxi.

'Hey,' I said. 'What is this?'

'Taxi, taxi,' he and the fat crook of a driver yelled at me.

'How much? How much?' I said.

'100 zlotys,' said the driver.

I didn't really care actually and allowed them to put me in.

The station was a fifteen-minute drive and seemed someway towards the end of the city. It also looked very small and very dirty. Could this be right? It looked more like a little suburban line station. At an inquiries desk a fat stupid woman looked at my ticket and shrugged. I said, 'Is this the right station?'

She pointed to the ticket and at a clock.

'Here?' I said. 'At this station?' pointing to my ticket and at the platform.

She nodded. I then looked at a notice-board and saw my train and the platform number. I got my things from the car and paid the driver. Soon I'd be sipping tea in my compartment and reading and relaxing.

I went to the platform. A number of people were waiting there. I had about half an hour to wait. Excellent. Soon a huge green Russian train heaved into the station. I was puzzled. It said Moscow/Berlin on it.

I went up to a fat Russian guard who reeked of cheap scent. 'Is this my train?' I said showing her my ticket. She looked at it blankly.

'Nyet,' she said — and then spoke in Russian, gesticulating vaguely. After a bit she took me by the arm and beckoned me to follow her. She led me to a superior sort of guard with red flashes on her uniform.

I looked almost fondly at the Russians. I felt I knew them. The new guard looked at my ticket. 'Gone,' she said. 'Too late.' She pointed at the time of departure.

'No,' I said. 'It's due in half an hour.'

'Too late,' she repeated stubbornly. The younger guard was looking at me sadly with her huge stupid eyes.

I looked at the ticket and my blood ran cold. I had read 13.49 as 3.49.

'Jesus!' I said. 'You're right.'

One part of me was furious with myself; another was quickly thinking what must I do? I could always try to return to the hotel and get the next train perhaps tomorrow but that was awful — I couldn't bear not to be on my way and anyway how would I find a taxi out here.

Someone said: 'Paris. Down there. Paris train.' 'Where?' I said. They pointed to a guard down the platform. I ran to him. 'Paris?' I asked.

'Da! Da!'

'Can you take me?' I asked showing him my ticket.

'Da! Da!'

Well, it seemed better than nothing. Paris — what a friendly, familiar place it sounded.

The Russian guard pointed to a carriage and nodded. I climbed aboard . . . .

GETTING HOME

I am on a train at a place called Frankfurt — not to be confused with another Frankfurt. This one is just inside East Germany. Having missed my lovely train at Warsaw — that would have taken me direct to the Hook of Holland — I simply got on the next one. As far as I could gather this train would take me to Berlin, West Berlin I hope and pray, arriving at about 12.00 midnight. But the Russian guard, although he was very friendly and even bought me a free unsolicited cup of tea, could not convince me I had been wise to board this train. I hope in a vague way that at Berlin I'll find some way to get to the Hook. I mean there must be trains — mustn't there? Jesus I hope so. Anyway at about 10.00 p.m. we arrived at some sort of border control. Guards got our passports checked, tourist visa bought and we rolled on. I dozed hoping the next stop but one or two would be West Berlin. In a way the longer we took the better for me. I didn't terrifically look forward to a night on an East Berlin station. The longer I spent in my compartment (with my travelling partner, a wonderful Pole) the better. Imagine my surprise when we were woken by the guards five minutes later and told, I think, that he was fucking off back to Moscow and we were all changing wagons.

Pandemonium broke out — old ladies wailing and protesting, workers tumbling out of bed and on to the platform jabbering away at each other, old men dithering, fat young women in pyjamas waving their arms and we, unable to speak any of their languages, very puzzled and getting a little alarmed. A French-speaking woman hopped up and down in front of the guard trying to find out what was going on. I discussed the situation with her for a bit but she got it into her head that each time I asked a question I was stating a fact. 'Is he telling us to get off the train?' turned into 'He's telling us to get off the train!' and so on.

127

I got off the train with my bags and asked some German railway people for the Berlin train. Things took a turn for the worse; in a sense they seemed to be saying the train for Berlin was the one I'd just got off. I clambered back on and confronted the Russian guard. He was carrying some very heavy luggage for a very old lady and exasperation bordering on fury was expressed in his eyes and tight mouth. 'Not *you* again,' he seemed to say with a savage look. We all seemed to be moving one carriage down rather than a more radical change to a new train — and that is the present state of affairs. I'm sitting between my Pole and an old Russian lady — at least I think she's Russian. I heard her muttering something about a 'kashmar' and I happen to know that's Russian for nightmare. The Pole just drank a can of beer and ate a foul-looking (and smelling) sausage. Now he is cleaning his teeth with his tongue and making loud explosive sucking noises.

Ah, we've just started moving again.

I wonder where to.

1.30 a.m.: We went on uncomfortably for an hour or so. Right now I am in Berlin — East I'm afraid, standing on a platform with a bunch of Armenians, one of whom is the French-speaking woman from the train. They seem to think we are waiting for the Paris train. It seems unlikely somehow. I have a nasty feeling she's waiting here because I am — we could be in an ongoing situation I fear.

I feel tired, ever so slightly headachy, and not quite as worried as I feel I should be. I meant to jot down the following thoughts on missing the train:

'FUCK!'

2.00 a.m.: still on the platform. It's getting chilly. I just got out a jersey and put it on.

All the Armenians are still here. There is an old man — he just came up and asked me is this East or West Berlin. When I said East, he pulled a face.

My Pole is standing patiently holding his bag. He looks as if he might as well be here as anywhere else. The train we came in on pulled out — another train came in. 'Good,' I thought, 'we're on our way.' But it turned out to be the Berlin–Moscow express. Nothing would get me on board *that*.

If a Paris train does arrive I think I'll stay on it to Paris. Or should I try to descend at Berlin West. Perhaps it won't stop in Berlin and my problems will be solved.

2.30 a.m.: The rather depressing news that the Paris train will get in at 6.00 a.m. has just come through. I do not look forward one bit to the next three-and-a-half hours. The Armenians, who are very angry in a cheerful sort of way, are settling down for the wait. I lay down for a bit

128

on a bench. The old lady came over and said I'd make myself ill lying down. 'Better to walk about, for the blood it's better.' I laughed and said, 'maybe'. After a very few minutes I had to get up — I was freezing. I was a bloody fool to get on that train. I should have gone back to the hotel and blown everything on a plane ticket. Oh well!

The longer this goes on and the more uncomfortable it is the more of a fool I feel.

One of the first sights I saw on this god-forsaken platform was a train pulling in with a young soldier, who'd forced open the sliding doors, leaning out and being sick. It pretty well sums up my feelings.

5.45 a.m.: Unbelievably awful night, freezing cold, very uncomfortable. I put on two pairs of socks, two jerseys, tried walking up and down, but very tired and cold, so curled up on hard bench. The Armenian came and told me he had discovered a buffet miles away underground. We went to look for it. It was warm but that's about all you could say for it. They wouldn't take our money but I had 1 mark (change from buying my transit visa). I bought one cup of coffee and shared it with the Armenian. We put sugar in it that I had in my pocket.

The buffet was full of exhausted miserable people — God knows who they were — wearily sitting out the night.

At 5.30 a.m. a grand looking train pulled in, was it the Paris express? was it bloody hell. The German guard told us the Paris train didn't come in until 7.20 a.m. On an impulse I asked if this train went to West Berlin. Ja! ja! I got on. Christ knows where it's going but at least with a bit of luck it will be out of this damned country. I threw my bags into an almost empty compartment. The only other occupant was my Pole.

6.50 a.m.: The world's worst tourist, exhausted, with no deutschmarks and a long wait ahead until 12.52 p.m. is sitting on some dirty stairs in Berlin's Zoo station and feeling ridiculously triumphant. I have to wait until 8.00 a.m. before I can cash a traveller's cheque. Then I'll ring home, have coffee, a very short walk and back here to get a train and I pray a night ferry.

The check coming across from the East was very cursory. No customs check, just a stamp on my visa.

Oddly enough the first impression of West Berlin is of filth; but filth and bustle, filth and colour and for me anyway the lifting of the corrosive anxiety that is permanently there in the Soviet Bloc. No more worries about visas and police nosing around one's notebooks or Solidarity badges. I could, if I knew how, fly home or fling myself on the mercy of some authority and expect them to help — more or less. It is true of course that I never had the slightest trouble from any authority in Russia or Poland but it was in the air — people warned about it.

The filth on this large station is a western kind. I've already seen those depressing little groups of drunks or dope addicts that cluster in western railway stations. I've seen a man rummaging in a litter bin. In a shop I entered to ask my way there were pornographic magazines as well as lists of newspapers, books, cigarettes, souvenirs, etc. I could imagine a Russian seeing it for the first time and being appalled. I made a few inquiries at the information desk. A somewhat surly girl told me what I wanted to know. She was no more polite — indeed much less polite — than her Intourist equivalent and yet . . . and yet I could have kissed her. She belonged to the same system I did. I understood her better than I understood any Russian.

There is also litter here and of course adverts. No boring boring busts of Lenin though; no signs reading: 'Chancellor Schmidt gloriously leads us ever forward in the struggle for peace.'

I dunno — I wish I was back in filthy old London.

I still feel slightly headachy and kind of chilled — like one does after a sleepless night on a freezing East German station. It rained all night, dripping through holes in the roof. Breath hung in the air.

On the way from East Berlin the train had stopped briefly at a customs checkpoint and we then crossed the Berlin Wall. What a monstrosity. In the early morning rain imagination could barely conceive a more dismal sight. Two caped soldiers patrolled the edge of what I supposed is a minefield — high blank walls, cold water, sentinel towers, wire. Vera in Leningrad told us it was defensive — built to keep out vandals. As if anyone who was not completely crazy could possibly want to break *into* East Germany. What a chilling sight; how inexpressibly dull.

11.15 a.m.: I'm so terrified of missing this train that, after my little walk-about including absolutely delicious breakfast — coffee, rolls, ham (smoked) and cheese — and a visit to excellent bookshop, I'm back at the station. Actually I'm feeling a bit too knackered to walk far. Never mind the filth and sex shops and garish adverts and difference 'twixt poverty and wealth. Never mind the litter — I'm back in the West, and I can stop off and eat or browse or window shop; I can feast my senses on glamorous women and smart cars and expensive-looking shops. There was a queue of about two people at the reservation counter — I thought 'blast . . . I'm going to have to wait.' Poor Poles, poor Russians, Bulgarians, East Germans, Czechs — 'poor' the whole lot of them, poor bloody sods.

It's rather odd that while I was in Russia I thought of the Russians as a downtrodden people and as persecutors simultaneously.

12.20 p.m.: The world's worst tourist, sweaty and tired, is sitting in a first class compartment on the train to the Hook. I sprang on board as the thing slowed to a halt — nothing can possibly go wrong — click! go wrong — click . . . .

A story Harry told me suddenly floated into my mind. An Englishman, Frenchman and an Irishman were cast away on a desert island. One day a genie in a bottle was washed ashore, they released him and he granted them each a wish. The Englishman wished to be in his club, about to go into dinner with a few close friends — phttt! and he was gone. The Frenchman wished to be in his girl-friend's flat about to share a bottle of champagne with her — phttt! and he was gone. The genie turned to the Irishman who thought for a moment: 'Shure oi don't know what oi want — but oi wish oi had me mates back.'

I had a lovely long drink of beer before getting on the train. Freezing cold and so refreshing.

An American journalist I met in Warsaw told me that once when she was travelling across East Germany last year the customs men had confiscated all her Solidarity literature and posters and badges. I hid mine therefore when I came through — though it proved unnecessary. How ludicrous it seems to hide such stuff here, or to think that this Government would give two prunes whether I'm crossing their country or not.

I had a marvellous train journey across West Germany and Holland. Very comfortable seats and I dozed and slept quite a bit. In between I read *Hamlet* and had lunch in a clean, efficient restaurant car and drank beer. I must have become very dehydrated because I drank three bottles of beer and two coffees.

I also chatted to a man who got into my compartment at one stop halfway across Germany. He said something to me I didn't catch and I said: 'I'm sorry I don't speak German.' 'I don't speak German either,' he said in a thick Liverpool accent. He was a working man, puffing on a roll-up cigarette and carrying a suitcase. He was an unlikely looking companion in a first class carriage. From a bulging plastic bag there protruded a builder's spirit level.

He had been on his third trip, I think, to Germany to work as a bricklayer. Building contractors over here frequently recruit workers from England and Ireland (as he put it 'from all over') for short working stints. As far as I could gather one of these itinerant workers, an Irishman, now has his wife and children with him, speaks competent German and is thinking of settling here.

This trip had been unfortunate for my acquaintance. He had gone for three weeks, leaving his wife, who works part time, and three children, (11, 8 and 4) at home. He is supposed to be paid whether he works or not but this time the work ran out after two weeks and the contractor would not pay him for the third week. As he was sending most of his money home this left him stranded and broke. He wired his wife to return some money and she tried to but it didn't arrive. In the end he went to the

British Consul. They were not too pleased to see him but gave him a first-class ticket back to England. He also went to some place I think he called 'The barnhof', where they provided him with soup ('not just a bowl — you could go back and back; eat as much as you like') and a huge packet of sandwiches for his journey. He was not too delighted with the sandwiches because they were made of very dark rye bread which he disliked. He gave me one later — it was delicious. Back in Harwich he has to report to the 'social' and get a ticket home. I asked if they'd just hand it over or would he at some time have to repay the cost. He thought they'd just hand it over. 'You couldn't do it too often mind.'

So after three weeks separated from his family and living out of a suitcase in some sort of hostel, having had the initiative to go so far to look for work, he's going back home, at the taxpayer's expense, flat broke.

It was an interesting story.

I said could I buy him a drink. Eagerness and embarrassment struggled comically on his face — he half rose but turned the movement into a sort of squirm and sank back. 'No,' he said bluntly, 'I wouldn't be able to buy you one back.' He spread his empty hands eloquently.

'That's OK,' I said, 'I've got some money and anyway I only want one. C'mon.'

'OK' he said.

We sat in the restaurant-car drinking. He said that Mrs Thatcher tells people to travel to find work, 'so I travelled, but I got ripped off'. He said he'd go on the dole when he got home. He did a day's work here, a couple there: 'You know, garden walls — little repairs. I hate repointing.' But he stayed on the dole: 'You can't come off it just to do one or two days work.' I wonder if the Tory Conference would therefore brand him 'a scrounger'. He is buying his council flat and has a mortgage. He says when he's out of work for a week or so he gets out of condition — when he starts work again.

'You don't half sweat you know — it really makes you breathe.' His brother, two brothers-in-law and his father-in-law are all unemployed at the moment. 'That's most of the family.'

As he came from Liverpool I asked him about the riots and what people thought of the Government's response. He knew quite a bit about plans for redeveloping dock areas and creating open spaces and marinas and so on. 'Do you think all this is a good idea?' 'I think people are in a "wait and see" mood! They just don't know,' he replied. About racial problems he said: 'Well I think people should be able to go where they want, you know, live and let live. So long as they don't come and live near me,' he added, going off into cheerful laughter. He recalled gang fights between Whites and Blacks when he was younger. 'I didn't get involved. We used to stand on the balcony of the flats and watch. Once the women in the flats — they knew the Black boys was coming and they knew they was coming under a sort of pass place. They prepared boiling water, you know in kettles and saucepans, and when the Black lads came through they poured it on 'em.'

'Christ!' I said. 'What happened?'

'They melted,' he said quick as a flash and laughing. 'You know — hot chocolate, drinking chocolate. No — but seriously — they didn't half shout!'

'Did they come back — for revenge?'

'Oh yeah! They come back of course — but they didn't come that way.' He quite frankly didn't want immigrants around. He will not allow his children to date coloured people when they get older. On the other hand, and mildly ironically, he would like to emigrate himself. Possibly to Australia — 'But my wife is not too keen. She'd like — you know — to sit it out.' He was quite fatalistic, calm, and even good natured as he told this sorry tale. He was not apparently white with rage and frustration. I would guess he's a good worker and family man. One of his childen is football mad and he was taking him home a football kit from Germany. He talked with pride about his work.

'A brick wall is . . . a *brick wall* . . . not a breeze block thing or slab of concrete!' He said he'd been given a lousy trowel to work with — the foreman noticed he was having difficulty with it and said 'How do you like that trowel?'

'I told him I didn't like it — I said,' here he dropped his voice. 'I told him "it's a cunt of a trowel".' So he had been given another — he mentioned its trade name as if to say — 'he gave me a Rolls Royce.'

The main work problem in Germany was they put too many 'brickies on the line'. Three men working together was OK. Seven or eight and it's impossible to keep the work even and looking good.

Early the following morning I took the ferry from the Hook of Holland to Harwich.

133

HUNGARY

Tuesday 14 May 1985

Crossing a border is exciting and some are more exciting than others. A couple of days ago I took a train from Victoria to catch an express that runs from Ostend to Vienna. Strolling through customs as I got off the ferry was not exactly thrilling but it was fun, and on the train across Europe I enjoyed handing over my passport from time to time to young uniformed officers who would glance at it for a moment or two and maybe raise their eyes to check the likeness of my passport picture. But that was all.

This afternoon after a short drive through Austria we arrived at the Hungarian border. Crossing a border into a Communist country is quite different. On the Austrian side the guards gave us the usual casual glance and waved us on. The day was very hot and ahead through a dusty haze lay the Hungarian check-point. As we approached it Harry and I agreed there was a special something in the air here, a certain 'I don't know what' about the place that raised our excitement. It may have been to do with the soldier in a watch tower who was gazing down at us. The giant size of the iron barrier that barred our progress affected our mood too. It was over a foot thick and looked as if it could have held up a tank. Behind it a soldier in khaki paced to and fro. Across his chest he nursed a squat gun. Harry said: 'It all looks ordinary enough but it's the real thing. His gun is loaded and if you tried to break through here he'd shoot you. It happened not so long ago; a lorry came through illegally. I think they shot one of the three men in it. He died later in hospital. The others made it.'

When the huge barrier lifted, worked I assumed by the man in the watch tower, we advanced to a passport check. The young man looked at mine and after a bit gave it back murmuring something in Hungarian. I frowned, puzzled, and he said in English 'Mother's name'. On my visa application I had written only my mother's maiden name in the slot where he needed her Christian name as well. I wrote Margaret and he took the papers back. After an extremely cursory look in the boot we were handed back our documents and politely waved on. Above our heads was a sign indicating certain regulations and things we should not be carrying into the country. One sign read 'PORNO' in bold black letters and in the last O, forming as it were the empty centre of the letter, was the silhouetted figure of a standing female nude, with one hand delicately raised.

There was no sudden change of countryside or architecture to notice as we drove towards Budapest. The same flat, well-tended fields rolled to left and right. Half the cars and lorries seemed to come from Austria.

Hitch-hiker

There were well-stocked stalls selling the fruit and vegetables and we passed a hypermarket that could just as well have been in France. It looked much the same as any modern European building. It was bright orange and hideous.

We passed a hitch-hiker and wondered whether to pick him up but didn't. He hadn't actually waved at our car (which has British number plates). 'Perhaps he wouldn't feel comfortable in a westerner's car,' said Harry. A mile or so further on we saw another hitch-hiker. This time he did thumb us down and Harry stopped. The man was still looking down the road away from us and made no move. Harry peeped the horn and as soon as he realized we'd stopped for him he trotted towards us and got straight in the back saying 'Budapest?'

He was a good-looking young man of perhaps twenty-seven years. He was bearded and wore casual clothes and carried no bag. It obviously made no difference to him at all whether he got a lift from a western capitalist or not. Harry began boldly to practise his limited Hungarian on our new companion.

He was on his way to an international football match, Holland versus Hungary, that was being played 150 kilometres away in Budapest. He was an electrical engineer and had been given his ticket by his company or group as a reward for good work. He had missed the works outing coach because he'd had to take his wife to see the doctor, because she was worried about not conceiving a baby.

He was extremely polite and good natured and spoke slowly to help Harry understand. He answered every question frankly and showed no interest whatever in us except to wonder why we were in his country and once when he saw my sketch-book he was amused to hear that I was a cartoonist.

I had noticed an enormous number of dead trees either side of the road as if Dutch elm disease had spread indiscriminately through all the spinneys and woods. He said: 'They are not blooming late, they are ill. It is acid rain.' At least that's how his answer came out in Harry's translation. I had read recently in English papers about pollution killing forests, but it had not prepared me for the sight of these hundreds and hundreds of dead grey trees rotting on the hillsides.

Now and then we passed extensive new building sites where, instead of high-rise blocks, small detached houses were being built. From the road I could not tell anything about the quality of the building but it was pleasant to see something other than hellish boxes going up for people to live in. Our hitch-hiker explained that this new building was being done privately. Young couples were helped to build their own houses with generous subsidies from the Government. They could get 40 per cent of the cost loaned to them at 3 per cent interest over thirty years. He also

136

told us that he got 6,000 forints per month, but by working privately out of hours he would usually double his income. His wife was an infant teacher and earned 3,000 forints per month and added 1,000 more by working overtime. If she had a baby the state would pay her 75 per cent of her salary for three years. If during that time she conceived again they doubled her pay. The young man gave us the impression that life was quite hard but that the mixture of private and official work was not a bad system. Several times he used a charming expression that summed up the way it worked. He would laugh and say of something or other: 'It is forbidden — but only a little bit forbidden.'

I noticed how buses and big lorries pulled over on to the hard shoulder of the motorway to let us pass and Harry remarked how polite the drivers were. He said: 'This would not be allowed in Austria.' 'It's not allowed here either,' said the hitch-hiker with a cheerful smile. He also warned

Harry to slow down because there were radar traps around, and other drivers passing in the opposite direction began to signal to us as well, and soon we passed a blue police car parked beside the road with various bits of electronic equipment sticking out of it.

We stopped at a parking spot beside the autobahn to look for Harry's Hungarian dictionary. The hitch-hiker was telling us that he had heard of English football hooligans. He had read in the papers that they attacked people and injured them and that they also attacked property. Harry could not think of the word for 'ashamed' to explain our attitude to our countrymen's reputation. When we arrived at the parking-place we found a small snack bar.

There were rows of salami sandwiches and various bits and pieces to eat and a little washstand. While we were there a coach full of football fans on their way to the game arrived and the place filled up swiftly with jostling men and several children. For a moment, because we'd been talking about hooligans, I felt myself tense up a little, but the crowd could not have been more harmless and good natured. I was trying to draw, which usually attracts attention when you do it in public. A few men craned to see what I was up to, then just smiled and looked away. They bought food and drink to carry away to their coach and soon the place was quiet again.

A sign announced that the snack bar was open twenty-four hours a day. The hitch-hiker told us it was privately owned. On the wall beside various advertisements in Hungarian for beer and so on was a familiar sign: 'Pepsi Cola. Have a good day.'

Outside, before we drove away, Harry said he wanted to see what the lavatory was like. It stood apart from the main building and looked like a little prefabricated hut. Moments later when he emerged Harry announced: 'Not bad — fine — clean — no criticism.'

When we had explained to the hitch-hiker that we had no money to pay for our drinks he'd said that we could change money unofficially here. It was only a little bit forbidden. We didn't because the rate was not much better than the official rate and it seemed too much trouble. Our two beers and a Pepsi came to about 70p.

One of the last things our friend told us before we arrived in Budapest was that he'd studied Russian all the time he was at school. It was a compulsory subject. Harry asked in the language: 'Can you speak Russian?' There was a snort of laughter and the young man replied in Hungarian. Harry laughed and translated. 'He said, he can just about say NYET.' This was the only time Russia or Russians were mentioned.

The hitch-hiker directed us to our hotel and shook hands before he left. Both Harry and I were struck by how straightforward, friendly and frank he'd been. He could have been Austrian, French, German or

English. So far we had had no experience apart from the border guard that set apart Hungary from anywhere in the West.

The Hotel Gellert was no exception. Built in curving *fin de siècle* style it was an imposing grey building overlooking the Danube near the Szabadság Bridge. Its huge concourse and quiet, polite staff created the most agreeable impression. Harry said: 'First we will visit the famous Hotel Gellert Thermal Baths, then we'll telephone a friend of mine and perhaps have dinner with him.'

I was shown to my lovely room. From a small balcony I looked over the river. There was almost no new building in sight, at least not high-rise building at all, which surprised as well as delighted me considering how much the city was knocked about in the war and during the 1956 revolution. The iron bridge and the shrieking trams, the low buildings and occasional spires and turrets all gave the view a 1920s look. It was like being inside a city scape by Max Beckmann and I could not have been more delighted with the place.

There was a knock on my door and Harry appeared dressed in a white

Hotel Gellert

towelling dressing-gown and carrying a towel. I put on the dressing-gown I found in my bathroom and followed him. I felt very naked and embarrassed walking through the hotel with so little on. This feeling increased when two young men quite ordinarily dressed got into the lift with us. But as we walked through the vast and lovely hall that led to the baths this awkwardness began to go. In niches between huge polished pillars were statues of nymphs. Many people dressed in almost nothing strolled in the great arched interior. The light was muted and all noise hushed by the size of the place.

Once inside we were directed to changing cubicles and emerged wearing nothing but small linen aprons tied absurdly behind in a little bow. Once in the steaming hot rooms where you could sit sweating and panting most people abandoned even their little aprons, but by then in the ferocious heat nudity didn't matter or seem remotely odd. The aprons were more peculiar really. In various rooms and interiors that gave off from the main way to the baths men were being massaged or taking showers or having pedicures or maybe just lounging and talking. Some were naked, some wore togas. There were slim young boys and hugely fat middle-aged men. Most appeared to be in a trance-like state of unawareness. Only one or two darted irritating looks as if considering one's appearance or figure with an eye to some more intimate acquaintance. A pair of self-conscious Dutchmen were the worst offenders at this. The older of them, bald and moustached, looked like the homosexual stereotype mocked by Michael Heath in his strip The Gays. He and his handsome young companion boldly flaunted their own relationship and looked us up and down. But I was really too hot to care much.

Inside the baths themselves the blue-tiled walls were richly decorated with sculpted figures and patterned mosaics. Daylight glimmered from above through thick glass panes. I tried to fix the scene in my memory because it was extraordinarily beautiful and strangely nostalgic. I'm not sure you can be nostalgic for something you've never had, or somewhere you've never been, but this place worked powerfully on me as if reminding me of a time, perhaps thousands of years before, when I had been very happy. I lay in the warm water and watched the other bathers slowly stepping in and out of the green-blue water. The colour of their pale skin created a pleasing harmony with the tiled walls and pale yellow and gold decorations. Gentle clouds of steam softened and blurred the picture until it almost melted into a dream. Some bathers chatted in half-submerged groups, some seemed to ponder on private thoughts alone and I lost track of time. It was long after seven before we went back to our rooms anyway. I don't know when I've ever felt so clean and relaxed . . . .

Later we drove out to find Harry's friend. We sat together with his

141

wife and passed a delightful evening drinking and eating. He was a middle-aged man, a scientist; his intelligent, chic wife was a lawyer. They had several children, one a doctor and at least one other a lawyer too.

The conversation ranged far, all in excellent English. Some was catching-up chat — 'How's the baby?' and so on; some was political; some comic; some moving, when for example there was talk of starvation during the war.

'For the last week I lived on dried carrots. That was all there was. Have you ever eaten dried carrots. . . ?' He shuddered and winced at the memory.

The picture of their country and its stage of development was fascinating. Here a Communist Government seems to have devised a system that was really quite extraordinarily free — by the standards of Eastern Europe I mean. Foreign newspapers were on sale. Citizens could travel frequently to the West. The private sector of the economy was very large. In June parliamentary elections would be held and candidates

142

did not have to be Party members. The only law seemed to be that every constituency was obliged to produce at least two candidates. (It was relatively easy for workers to join the Party but for members of the intelligensia, that is to say doctors, lawyers, teachers etc., it was difficult; their numbers were rationed as it were. This seemed to be an attempt to keep the Party a workers' party, but there was a kind of nonsense here because in a classless society, which after all is the aim of a Communist Government, the difference between doctor and labourer should have in one sense gone. However I failed to get this point cleared up.) The attitude to the Government could be summed up by a remark made by our host's wife.

'Here, now the Government is not considered our enemy any more. We have many problems but we know what they are. It is better that we should know. We understand more why things are as they are.'

For all this there was, nevertheless, another presence as it were in these conversations. It was the knowledge that the State had immense power and could and would use it ruthlessly if it felt it had to. And lurking behind everything else were the contemptible but frightening Russians. They were distant now and in many ways irrelevant, but their empire had the ability and the potential to afflict terribly the lives of all citizens. In the recent past and elsewhere they had proved that over and over again. However cheerful and resourceful and hopeful our hosts were, and they were all these things everywhere in the Eastern Bloc, if you kept your senses alert you were always aware of a disagreeable whiff of fear.

Before we left our host said to me: 'Please, if you should write anything about our conversation when you get home, do not mention my name.'

I read to Harry the last paragraphs I had written. He said yes, that was very fair. He then added his own description of the Russian presence here and all over the Eastern Bloc.

'The Russians are the restraining factor. They are like a wall that surrounds all their satellites. They allow people to run around relatively freely inside but no one must approach let alone touch the wall.'

He went on to qualify the picture of Hungary we had got from the scientist and his wife by pointing out that this was a family who had done very well by the system. They had their large city house and a country house too. He travelled freely in the West and really had little to complain about. Harry didn't mean the man was a liar, but. . . .

I said there was a saying I learnt in India: 'A dog with a bone in his mouth does not bark.'

Harry laughed. 'Exactly,' he said. 'Why didn't you say that to him?'

'I didn't think of it — anyway it's a bit rude.'

'I'd have said it,' he declared.

He mentioned another acquaintance of his he'd met on his last visit.

'He gave me a very rosy picture of the Communists, but I learnt later he's quite a liberal, almost a sort of dissident. Perhaps he thought the hotel where we met was bugged.'

'So why meet in a hotel?' I asked.

'Dunno, he suggested it.'

'Perhaps he knew it was bugged and was deliberately giving a good performance.'

'Yes perhaps — on the other hand if they knew that he knew it was bugged they would have seen through that.' We laughed and gave up this subject. I noted it down as an example of how one's mind started to work behind the Iron Curtain. Even here in relatively free and liberal Hungary.

Wednesday 15 May

I woke early and looked at the sun sparkling on the Danube and at the beautiful Szabadság Bridge. The yellow trams looked bright and gay in the hazy heat. The streets were already busy at 7.00 a.m.

After breakfast we walked in the blazing sunshine across the bridge to visit a large indoor food market.

In France during summer holidays I had often stood in market places and delighted in the wonderful richness and variety of produce that the French farmers brought for sale. I had a favourite fantasy of bringing some awful little Soviet aparachik to such a market and saying: 'Look, look at what the poor downtrodden, starving, brutalized masses of the West have to live on. See how they are ground down and starved by their masters.'

This fantasy would not work on a Hungarian because the market was full of produce and busy queues of people were buying it. It was for all the world just like France. There were apples and cucumbers, peppers and potatoes, carrots, turnips, cauliflowers and great spreading boxes of strawberries.

We wandered around for an hour or so. We bought walnuts and strawberries and enjoyed the place very much.

There was not only food for sale. You could also buy some clothes and baskets, crockery, drinks and cigarettes. It was a handsome old market. I could not understand how so many obviously nineteenth-century buildings had survived the battles that had raged across this lovely city. I must ask someone about this.

We drove to the Art Gallery and looked at the paintings. There were a number of very fine pictures. I was particularly pleased to see a Monet

portrait of a woman on a sofa, several superb Goyas (one I specially liked of a girl with a terracotta jug), an excellent Toulouse-Lautrec of some women sitting by a mirror. I rate Lautrec higher and higher as I get older. He was one of my first heroes and he gets better every year. There were several fine Velasquez's, but for me, best of all, a Corot portrait of a young woman in blue.

When we emerged from the gallery the brilliant hot day had completely altered and huge storm clouds were piling up in the sky. The air was heavy. Harry was keen to find a particular restaurant called The Apostles Restaurant. (It's just behind the Intercontinental Hotel right by the Elizabeth Bridge and very good if anyone wants to know.)

As we nosed slowly down a narrow busy street looking for the place a sudden flurry of activity caught our attention. A young man was grabbing at a young woman in a way that was clearly not playful. He tried to put her in a half nelson and seemed to want her to get into a car that was parked nearby.

'What's going on there?' said Harry. Almost before I had taken in the scene he was out of the car and advancing on the struggling couple. I followed him at once and as we hurried up Harry called in English: 'Hey! What's going on? What are you doing? Leave her alone!' He tapped the young man hard on the shoulder and the girl slipped to one side and walked rapidly away. The man instantly chased her, shouting and once more reached out to grab her. Harry hurled himself on the man and violently threw him to the ground. The attack was so sudden, confident and vicious that it took me completely by surprise. The young man, already in a blind fury, obviously wondered what on earth had hit him. He picked himself up and looked around. I moved between him and the girl and Harry stood alongside. The fellow was not big, smaller than me and Harry is at least six foot, fit and well built. The man, beside himself with rage, started forward once more still bellowing.

'Leave her alone,' I said and realized I had doubled up my fist. I supposed that the next thing might be an exchange of blows. The man stopped, looked at me then at Harry and screamed in German, as if it explained everything: 'It's my wife!' 'Das ist meine Frau!'

'So what,' said Harry, still for some reason speaking English — although he is completely fluent in German.

Suddenly the incident was over. The man walked back to his car, occasionally calling out over his shoulder and the girl hurried away. We also returned to our car, several mildly amused drivers waited for us to move on as we had blocked the road.

'Extraordinary business,' said Harry.

'Mm,' I said, full of admiration for his sudden and decisive act.

'Now where's that restaurant?' he said.

'Perhaps we should ask him,' I suggested, pointing to the man who was by now beginning to drive off in pursuit of his wife.

Harry laughed.

'What would you have done if he'd attacked you?' I said.

'He wouldn't have done,' he replied, 'He wouldn't attack two of us.'

'Suppose he had — he was very angry — would you have clouted him?'

'I dunno — probably not — sort of beaten him off — unless I'd had to hit him.'

'How long is it since you hit someone?'

'Oh God — mm. . .'

'Weeks and weeks,' I suggested.

'Mm — it must be — days and days ago.'

After lunch we walked round the centre of Budapest looking in shops and stopping often to admire the buildings. There was a heavy, sometimes lightly decorated, nineteenth-century building here which I liked very much. It was awfully hard to say why it was so pleasing. Something to do with the fact that much of it looked in rather bad repair, and there is nothing so romantic as faded grandeur. But it must also be noted that a great many of these buildings (the ones I am talking about are mainly offices now I suppose, with shops on the ground floor) were very well restored and neatly painted.

We also drove around in the suburbs a bit but saw nothing of great interest except that we noticed how much building was going on. Large, rather ugly expensive-looking villas were being built, at least in the area we passed through, in quite considerable numbers.

In the late afternoon we hoped to visit the Thermal Baths again but it turned out to be a women's day. While the women's side of the baths was being renovated the sexes took turns in the men's side.

Harry went for a swim in the ordinary pool and was whistled at by an attendant and called out because he was not wearing a bathing cap. I went to my room to look at the Bridge and write.

At 7.00 we met Éva, the sister of one of Harry's friends in Vienna. A psychologist, she has studied psycho-analysis and was in the final year of her medical training. She spoke very good English. We began to talk over a drink about the Tavistock Clinic where my wife works. Éva knew of the Tavistock of course and I said I was extremely surprised to hear that she could be psycho-analysed behind the Iron Curtain or that she could practise psycho-analysis here. In Russia psycho-analysis is not recognized as a useful technique; perhaps one could almost say not allowed. Its emphasis on the individual and the personal could not exist alongside a collective attitude to people. Problems in a Communist country are State problems and they are caused by some community

148

Post Office Budapest

breakdown, not because of some difficulty or unresolved battle or loss located in remote childhood.

She described the way she practised analysis and, from what my wife had taught me, I could ascertain that what she was able to do was pretty primitive. But her enthusiasm and eagerness were very clear. She said that the authorities looked with no kindness upon the practice of analysis but did not go so far as to actually forbid it. She had no trouble getting books on analysis. Freud's work was available in libraries and so on. But I could feel that without more contact with training of the kind that is available in the West her progress would be limited. Or perhaps she and her colleagues would develop an Eastern European brand of analysis independent of western traditions. She said she found much of what she read from the West too dogmatic. I wanted to ask her two things about Hungary and she said: 'Go ahead.' The first was did she know how much Budapest was knocked about by the war. I asked because I was so struck by being in a nineteenth-century city here. It was not until you got out into the edges of the city that it began to look really twentieth century. I didn't mean the cars and shop windows, but the wide streets and ageing façades of the buildings. She replied frankly that she just didn't know. She was I would guess in her late twenties and far too young to remember. She said she'd heard there was a lot of damage but not a real plastering like Warsaw suffered or Dresden.

The second thing I wanted to know was what she knew or thought about the parliamentary elections we'd been told were to be held in June. She frowned slightly. 'The elections,' she said. 'Yes.' 'What do you mean you want to know about them?'

'Well, we were told that anyone could stand, even non-party members. . . .'

She interrupted, laughing with obvious genuine amusement.

'Who told you that — it is a joke. The elections are a joke. It's not serious. . . .' She began to give us a completely different, and I'm bound to say much more plausible, picture of the proposed elections.

She did not know why the Government had decided to pretend to have elections but they had. Instead of 'elections' with one candidate, which has been the habit, from now on there must be at least two. Local meetings were called to choose the candidates and large industries were told to send large groups of workers to pack the meetings, which everyone knew were nonsense and therefore would not have attended. When people tried to take advantage of these meetings to go to them with a really independent candidate they were not allowed into the hall. They would be told by police that the hall was full, all places having been booked or that some absurd technical hitch prevented them from entering. This had happened to some of Éva's friends. When they

GUNDEL Restaurant
Budapest

complained later they were told yes, they should have been allowed in. Unfortunately that particular meeting was very badly organized and irregularities occurred. It was a regrettable mistake and of course those responsible had been disciplined and so on. But the decisions taken by the meeting stood.

Meanwhile, before the public meeting a private meeting of officials had already arranged a list of candidates. These could be voted for openly at the main meeting but it mattered not to the Government who went forward as a candidate because every single one of them was a party hack.

This sorry tale she told, expressing a mixture of amusement at the crassness of it all and contemptuous anger as well.

The elections were a sham put on for an obscure reason and everyone knew it. She asked who on earth could have given us any other

152

impression. When Harry told her she shrugged, obviously puzzled as to why such people should try to mislead us so. 'Perhaps', I said, 'because he had a good job and the system worked well for him, so why criticize it.'

'I have a good job,' she replied evenly. 'I have a flat and good prospects. The system "works well" for me too.'

'Perhaps', I went on, 'he is tired, he has seen too much fighting, too much destruction. Perhaps he's had enough.'

'Perhaps he has,' she said. She was able to convey the sturdy impression that she had only just begun. She was an exceptionally intelligent young woman, and motivated obviously by the highest ideals. The sort of person who should be her country's greatest pride, not its enemy. In the presence of such people you felt the full weight of the stupid awfulness of this abominable system.

Later on we talked about doctors. She told us that all patients paid doctors. They don't have to and they were not supposed to but they did. Because everyone knew they did doctors' pay was held very low to make up for it. Consequently doctors could barely live on their salary and had to accept the money many of them intensely disliked taking. When doctors were ill and could not work and had to take a pension they were in deep trouble because their pension was calculated as a proportion of an already tiny wage.

I asked how the money actually changed hands and who set the amount. She said different doctors and hospitals had different arrangements. Sometimes they would only accept something after the treatment was concluded so that they demonstrated their impartiality. Some people were just too poor to pay and they would get equally good treatment. Mostly people paid what they could in the hope always that a good payment would mean closer attention from the doctor.

Taxi drivers' and hairdressers' salaries were held ridiculously low for the same reasons — and many other professions as well.

'Life here is not clean, all is dirty,' said Éva.

Later she told me, trying to explain more: 'We are forced to break laws. The laws are bad and often unkeepable — nevertheless breaking them makes you feel bad. We suffer from a permanent sense of guilt.'

She talked of these matters with humour, anger, irony, courage and determination. She confronted and dealt with politics every day of her life in a way that was extremely difficult for us in the West to understand. Such talk produced in me a particular mood or reaction. I felt I was in front of veterans of battles I had never fought and would never have to. I felt therefore a gulf between us that was almost unbridgeable. One could reach out to such veterans and they would take your hand and be very friendly, but you both knew that when you turned away to return to your country the worst you would face would be someone such as Jim Callaghan or Norman Fowler or Margaret Thatcher or Neil Kinnock while they turned back to something very, very different.

Such Eastern Europeans were not much interested in our politics. They had no meaning or relevance. I asked Éva whether there was a feminist movement here. She replied that while there might be some matters that such a movement might address itself to, there were other more pressing issues that she felt had to be dealt with first. Harry asked her if she meant that a feminist movement was in a way a kind of luxury. Éva said that she felt that was true in a way but really women had equality in many ways. Most doctors, most lawyers, most teachers were women. There were almost no female politicians of high rank. Surgeons tended to be male. She said an English feminist had visited her in Budapest and tried to awaken in her enthusiasm for feminism. Éva laughed: 'I couldn't understand what she was so worked up about.'

Because of my interest in her country and its politics she asked whether I'd like to meet a friend of hers who could tell me more. She didn't know whether or not he'd talk to us, but when I said I'd like to meet him she said she'd try. Before we parted we arranged to telephone her on Saturday evening when we returned from Pécs to see if she had contacted her friend.

Thursday 16 May

We left for Pécs after a leisurely breakfast. It was very hot and as usual Budapest looked busy and cheerful in the sunshine. At least that was true of the centre; out towards the edge of town in an industrial suburban belt that we passed through the streets didn't look quite so jolly. But then the outskirts of big cities never did. One could not help making these sort of comparisons however meaningless they were. There were almost no signposts and it was difficult to be certain that we were on the right road and once or twice we stopped to ask. When we did at last come out into open country it looked much the same as country does look. There is no such thing as a Communist tree. The flat farmland was without hedges or fences and the prairie-like fields went on for ever.

The only indication that we were as far east as we were was when we passed a village and noticed bare dirt roads between the small houses. The sight had the effect of suddenly whipping one back in time into the nineteenth century. Only the few Lada motor cars parked on the mud challenged this illusion.

Ahead of us Harry caught sight of a woman walking along the side of the road. She was wearing black trousers and a white blouse and she was carrying what looked like plastic shopping bags. Her back was to us and she neither thumbed a lift nor even looked round. There were no houses in sight and the road swept on into the distance without a bend or a turning.

'I wonder if she'd like a lift,' said Harry. He has a way of acting at the same moment as he thought and stopped the car some yards ahead of the woman.

'Surely she won't get into a car with two men — foreigners at that?' I said.

'Dunno — she might,' said Harry turning and looking back. The woman was still walking on. She had not altered her pace or looked up, but as she drew alongside the car she opened the back door, placed her things in the car and got in.

She was a good-looking woman aged about thirty to thirty-five, deeply tanned by the sun and her dark curly hair was just flecked with grey. She wore no jewellery or make-up and spoke in a strong confident voice. She was returning to her workplace on a state-owned Agricultural Combine where she was employed by the Government as a farm worker. It turned out that her Combine was enormous, with many departments separated by hundreds of kilometres. She had been shopping nearby for seeds and gardening equipment. Although she had a car it was too expensive to use if only one person was going to town, so she either took a bus or hitch-hiked.

Her husband worked at another place. He was not a farm worker but seemed to be employed in some sort of office job.

She got four weeks' holiday a year and had visited Czechoslovakia and Yugoslavia. A few kilometres down the road some soldiers directed us off our route round a diversion and she explained there were army manoeuvres going on. These were not Russian soldiers although there were plenty of Russians around. They had forints to buy things with. Some even spoke a little Hungarian and had been here three to four years. Contacts were permitted and she knew of girls who had married Russian soldiers. She did not speak of Russians with any sign of resentment.

In her opinion the peasants were better off than the town workers. She worked on a dairy farm taking 10,000 litres of milk a day and processing or checking it somehow.

'Some milkmaid,' said Harry.

'Ask her if we can visit the farm,' I said, and she replied at once that we were welcome to come and look at the animals. After twenty minutes or so we arrived at a turning. To the right was a red painted arch, built of scaffolding surmounted by a large red star: to the left a track led away into the fields down which she directed us. After a few yards we stopped and walked towards a herd of cows that were being tended by a shirtless man whose bicycle leant against a hay wagon.

The day was fine and summery. The grass cool and lush. The cows looked contented as cows will. I began to draw them. Our guide tapped me gently on the shoulder, and when I looked up she pointed at the drawing and then at herself.

'She wants you to give her a drawing.'

'OK.'

They waited while I drew for a few minutes. Then I showed her the drawings and asked her to choose one.

'She says she wants any one,' said Harry.

So I tore one from the book. I asked her her name which was Papp Mária and wrote a little dedication to her then gave it to her. She took it and said something to Harry who replied in English 'Thank you'. 'Thank you,' she said to me in a matter of fact way.

Back in the car Harry said he would drive Mária to her house and we crossed the road passing under the red star and down a tree-lined dirt track.

To the left there were several new houses going up. Mária said: 'It is easy to build if you work here, the State helps you. Unfortunately I'm building socialism at the moment and haven't yet built my home.' We all laughed, and moments later with a look of glee on his face Harry said: 'She has invited us for coffee — do you want to go?'

156

Kitchen garden *अल्लुरितम् (?)*

Agricultural Cuisine

'Yes.'

Harry had not been able to understand every word she spoke but the gist of her invitation was: 'If you do not mind coming to my very simple house I would like to offer you some coffee.'

The dirt-track wound on through the trees, passed dwellings and barns and over a small river. The pot holes got worse and worse and at last we came to a row of low houses. Each had a small garden and fence in front of it and women sat in the sun. Several of them were preparing food I think.

Mária pointed out her place and got out to open a gate. She gestured to Harry to drive in.

When we got out of the car a dreadful-looking Alsatian guard dog strained towards us on its chain, barking, and three furry black puppies came galloping out yapping at us as well.

Behind the house there was a garden with rows of onions, cabbages, carrots, tomatoes and strawberries. There were several fruit trees too. Washing was hanging from two lines and exactly similar gardens could be seen either side, and beyond the gardens there were more houses and outbuildings.

Mária took us into her small poor kitchen. The interior was not dirty but not clean either. It was very bare and yet untidy. The walls were white and decorated with three black-flowered plates and a piece of embroidered cloth pinned at an angle on the wall. There was a fridge, a cupboard and a table with two chairs and a stool. The stove was off the little kitchen or parlour and another door led into the house. Mária disappeared through one to make coffee, and a large, sleepy, smiling woman appeared from the other. She was a little younger than Mária and appeared to have just got up because she was lazily tucking in her T-shirt and doing up her belt. She was called Elizabeth and was Mária's younger sister. After a few moments yet another young woman appeared. This one was about sixteen and was carrying a toddler. She was one of Mária's three daughters and the baby belonged to a neighbour. From next door (the two houses were joined and shared a back porch) came very loud English pop music. It was the worst kind of clack, clack, clack, bash, bash, bash, ow, ow, ow, kind of rubbish.

After shaking hands with us Elizabeth and the teenager vanished and when they came back a few minutes later Elizabeth was wearing a different top and the girl had put on quite a bit of scent.

When the coffee came Mária and Elizabeth talked and we learnt more. Mária worked from 5.00 a.m. to 11.00 a.m., then came home to make lunch and rest. Her next shift was 4.00 p.m. to 9.00 p.m. She did five days on and five days off. She came from Pécs. One of her daughters worked in Budapest and the youngest was at boarding school. The local school was no good. It only went up to the fourth year and was run by a married couple who taught everything.

Her husband no longer lived with her — they separated two years ago when she came to work on the farm. In this department there were about 250 workers. She did not care too much for her neighbours because they were dull and poorly educated. They were also nosey. One woman would become ill if she did not find out all about her visitors!

The farm was well run by a strict but fair manager (Mária gestured with her fist). The land was fertile and, as her pay was related to her productivity, her basic 4,200 forints per month was often made up to 7,000.

This, said Harry, was presumably the secret of Hungary's agricultural success. He recalled the market in Budapest bursting with produce. The farmers had a clear incentive to do well.

Elizabeth told us she had spent three months in France recently staying with friends in Paris and Lille. She brought up a little photograph album and showed us pictures of herself snuggling in the arms of various smiling young men — one showed her in front of the Eiffel Tower. She had been given permission to go abroad for one month, but she stayed away for three. Her punishment was that she was not allowed to travel abroad for three years. Permission was usually given annually for foreign travel.

She knew what her punishment would be and now regretted that she didn't obey the law. Three years seemed an awful long time to her.

Harry said: 'You must stay here and build socialism.' She replied 'Mm. I'm not even allowed to visit a socialist country though.'

Mária's daughter did not join in the conversation. She was a dark pretty creature like a little vixen. She leant against the fridge and smoked cigarettes, letting the smoke drift out of her open mouth. All three women petted the toddler as he staggered in and out, picking him up and cuddling him affectionately.

We were offered food and given thick slices of bread covered in some sort of pâté with dashes of red paprika sauce on top. They looked very pretty but were very filling so I could only eat two. Mária picked up the plate and thrust it at me urging me to take more. I couldn't. Harry got through three but he secretly grimaced at me as if to say it was quite an effort.

Harry was charming the women to bits. The atmosphere was extremely pleasant. I asked if I could see the garden and was taken on a little tour and I stopped to do some drawing.

It did not surprise me at all when we were invited to stop for a meal on our way back to Budapest in a couple of days. We accepted with pleasure and before we went Mária shook her finger at Harry and said: 'Is it certain, 100 per cent certain, that you will come on Saturday?' and Harry smiled and said: 'Yes, 100 per cent certain.'

Mária was anxious about whether we could find our way through the twisting lanes back to the road but we assured her that we could.

We shook hands and thanked them warmly. As we drove away the teenager stood by the car window and spoke for the first time. 'Hello,' she said.

'Hello,' I said. 'Hello.'

We drove through the hot afternoon delighted with this meeting. I congratulated Harry for setting it up.

'You have a kind of genius for making things happen.'

161

We discussed the women at some length, unable to make out what their attitude to us was, whether it had a romantic element or was pure friendly curiosity. After all it was not every day that a Hungarian-speaking Englishman came into their life and, to put it bluntly, Harry was exceptionally charming. But the whole episode was so casual,

soldiers in cafe

Kalocsa

friendly and frank, it seemed impossible to believe that they were setting up some sort of assignation. But then why had Elizabeth gone and changed her shirt?

'And she had no bra on,' said Harry thoughtfully.

The countryside remained flat and the villages we passed through were quite pretty and looked unmodernized.

Our stop with Mária had made us very late. We had to be in Pécs by 6.00 in order to find the addresses of the rooms we had booked through the tourist office. We had discovered that all the hotels were full. Once we tried to cross the Danube by a ferry to shorten our journey. In the late afternoon light the river was inexpressibly beautiful. Several rowers were sculling past, disturbing the surface of the water, and on the far distant bank the dark green trees were reflected even darker in the river. Swallows flew in the still air and a couple with a small child were sunbathing near where we stopped. We discovered that there was a two-hour wait for the next ferry and decided to drive on.

I would have liked to stay but we couldn't. In the end realizing we'd never make it to Pécs we found a hotel in Baya. I was quite delighted with it and the large square that our rather grubby little room overlooked.

BAYA

We drank beer out of doors by a small river and later took a stroll through the town looking for a restaurant. We did some window-shopping and at last asked an elderly couple if they could direct us to a restaurant. They pointed across the river and added the word 'MASZEK' and burst out laughing. Their amusement was conspiratorial and genuine. They were telling Harry that the restaurant they were guiding him to was privately owned, and by implication of better quality than the rest.

Actually it turned out to be an awful modern place and we finished up in a cheerful little bistro down by the river where a gypsy band played very loudly. . . .

Friday 17 May

Before leaving Baya in the morning we looked around the shops trying to find something for our families. It is at such moments that you become aware of the dullness behind the architectural charm of a little town like this. A toy shop offered almost no choice, and what there was for sale was tawdry, ill made and cheap. Cheap simple toys can often be the best and the prettiest, but these were tatty plastic and looked as if they'd fall apart at once. We didn't buy anything.

On the way to Pécs we stopped for a coffee at Mohásc. We sat by the Danube and watched a car ferry crossing over the river. A man was scything the grass on the bank near us and on the balcony was a group of three men playing cards. One came over to us and said in halting German that, as he had seen me drawing, he was interested to learn what the price would be for a sketch of him and his friends playing cards.

I said: 'Two cups of coffee.'

I noticed that Harry translated it as doubles or large cups of coffee. 'I drive a hard bargain,' he said. 'It's your first commission — you'd better make it good.'

'I'll try.'

'One day some art dealer will see your drawing pinned up in his house and say: "My God, do you know what you've got there?" '

' "Yeah," he'll say, "That's a genuine Garland, from the Mohásc period if I'm not mistaken." '

The card-player brought us two single coffees and sat down again while I began drawing. He got up again and I called out: 'Hey! sit down, old man. You can't go yet.' Harry said to him in German: 'You can't move 'till he's finished.'

'I'm just getting some beer.'

'You must wait.' He sat down, pulling a comical wry face.

When I'd finished Harry took the drawing over to the men, who

Mohásc. By the Danube

studied it, laughing. Harry said: 'One of them is saying you've given his
friend a bigger beard than he's actually got — "You've done him
proud".'

As we left one of the men took the drawing into the café to show some
women and I heard a burst of laughter.

Before we left Mohásc we stopped to visit the museum. Here, and in
Baya, Harry had noticed street signs and posters in several languages
including German and Croat. He wanted to know if some minority
groups lived around this area. The museum turned out to be about the
Turkish invasion of Hungary in the sixteenth century. It was here that
Suleiman II defeated and destroyed the Hungarian army. There were
weapons and pots and bits of armour and so on and some pictures of
terrible battles. Suleiman seems to have been a bit of a rough diamond.

The lady in charge of the museum confirmed that there were indeed
the local minority groups that Harry had suspected were here.

As we drove on towards Pécs I said: 'You know, I feel I am cheating my paper. Things are not hard and uncomfortable and frightening around here. It's not like the Soviet Union or Poland. Most of the time I am more or less unaware that I'm in a Communist country.'

'Mm, I know what you mean. But it *is* a Communist country. There are plenty of Russians around, it's just that you don't see them because they are hidden in their camps.'

'Perhaps we could go and see them.'

'Mm, why not.'

'Couldn't we ring up their Press Office and ask?'

'You mean ask to speak to their P.R. officer and say that you're a visiting journalist from a right-wing English newspaper and that you'd like to go to a typical Russian military camp or depot?'

'Yes, just to talk to the soldiers and do some drawings of any installations or buildings there.'

'Anything in particular you'd like to draw?'

'Oh no, — just what was there.'

'Nothing secret or sensitive.'

'Good heavens, no.'

'You'd like to go to the sort of Russian camp that was open to the Hungarian public?'

'Mm absolutely.'

'Well, why not.'

We often amused ourselves with this sort of joke. In Pécs we saw a magnificent municipal building. Put up some time during the monarchy, it was beautifully decorated with sculpted figures, and right up to its elegant towers it was newly painted in yellow ochre with paler cream on its pillars and window frames. It looked superb. Above the pointed roof of its highest tower some bloody fool had put a large red plastic star, which glowed at night.

'Look, up there.'

'Oh. Isn't that great. Is it original?'

'It's magnificent, but I don't think it's original.'

'Perhaps not, but it's just what that building needed. Just that little touch, to bring it to life.'

'It's extraordinary isn't it — once you've seen how *right* it is — it's hard to imagine the building without it.'

'It seems to blend. . . .'

'And it looks so — I don't know — friendly.'

'Comforting. . . ' etc., etc., etc.

When we arrived in Pécs quite hungry at about 1.30 p.m. we tried a hotel instead of the tourist office and as they had a room after all we took it. Right by the hotel was a large squat mosque; its minarets were gone but it was a powerful reminder of the time the Turks were here long ago. The mosque was now a church and inside, awkwardly crammed between the delicate Muslim arches, were positively awful statues of Christ and the Virgin and one of a soppy-looking monk holding an even soppier-looking child. In a mosque the twisted figure on a crucifix suddenly looked like a sado-masochistic nightmare.

There was a mural of a beaten Turk warrior and over him loomed an armoured Hungarian Knight incongruously supported by a monk looking all radiant. I had never been absolutely potty about the Turks — they seemed to have been involved in more than their share of brutality over the years — but the inside of this place warmed me to them, or at least their religion.

After lunch we went shopping and once more found nothing. We tried a big department store the equivalent of a Waitrose or Tesco supermarket. There was no shortage of anything that we could see. Well-stocked freezers with chickens and what looked like goose or turkey, row upon row of canned and bottled food and the usual washing powders and household goods. Upstairs there were clothes, shoes and bits of equipment such as fridges and cookers.

The difference between this place and its western equivalent was not hard to feel but more difficult to convey.

There was an overall dullness, and in spite of there being plenty of everything there was almost no choice. Perhaps because there was no competition between makes of say washing powder, no attempt was made to package it attractively or display it temptingly. This did not result in a quiet and ordered simplicity but in a careless kind of drabness. Nothing was displayed well — for example, some of the shoes were thrown into bins for shoppers to sift through. Not thrown there as part of a special offer, to get rid of them, but simply on sale. Fairly quickly the inner dreariness of the place had a tremendously depressing effect, at least it did on me and Harry. If I were a Socialist it would worry the hell out of me.

Out in the street again, still having bought nothing, we came to a large and beautiful synagogue. Inside an elderly man was renting out little guide pamphlets. He had an immensely attractive manner. He was thin, aged in his late sixties and he wore a suit and an ordinary gent's hat on his head. He talked to us in a quiet voice in a mixture of English, German and Hungarian telling us when services were held and so on. He had a strangely soothing personality and I wanted to speak to him longer but a group of Hungarian tourists came in and he broke off to deal with them. He laid his hand on Harry's arm and, referring to our pamphlets, asked him to point out any errors in the English.

The synagogue was in quite good repair and the knowledge that it was

167

Pécs

Woman
came out & said
There are Gypsies living here

still there and busy moved me very deeply.

In the guide I read that upstairs there were 448 seats where women used to sit and downstairs there were 476 seats for the men. Of the 4,500 Jews who lived in Pécs before the war only 464 remained, so now both men and women sat downstairs, the men on the right and the women on the left. It seemed to me they sat closer to each other for comfort. Immovably secured to the Torah reading table was *The Book of Tears*, in which were inscribed in alphabetical order the names of all the Jews lost during the Second World War.

I said to Harry we should try to talk to the old man tomorrow if we could.

A little while later as I was queuing in a toy shop to purchase a little nonsense for one of my children, I noticed that the woman serving me had a number tattooed on the forearm. I had seen photographs of such tattoos but never actually seen one before. Conflicting emotions of rage against her persecutors and some sort of admiration for her because she survived sprang up in me. I felt a desire to communicate this to her somehow while I knew that that was quite impossible. She talked animatedly to a well-fed young man for a few moments who was not a shopper but a friend perhaps or even her son.

We found ourselves by our hotel and went in for a coffee in the buffet. We wrote postcards and I drew. Some time later I realized Harry was not there and vaguely looking around for him saw him across the far side of the room earnestly talking to the manager. He saw me looking at him and he waved a hand and grinned as if to say 'wait a minute'. I thought: 'What's he cooking up.' Late afternoon sunlight filled the large comfortable room. The place was busy but not crowded. There was a pleasant murmur of talk and laughter.

Harry sat down at our table again and announced 'I've had to resort to violence again.'

'What do you mean.'

'Well, you know, exert my authority, show 'em what's what.'

'What are you talking about?'

'Well, it's a very strange story. Just now I went to the loo. You know how you might — felt like having a pee.'

'Yes, I know what you mean.'

'Mm, well I went downstairs and in the loo, perfectly ordinary loo cubicles and little pissoirs. . . '

Yes! Yes!'

'Well in the loo was a boy snogging with a girl.'

'Really.'

'Yes. I waited for a moment — bit surprised — I expected them to go now that they weren't alone. Not a bit of it, they just stood there.'

169

'What did you do.'

'I said, in English, "Do you mind leaving".'

'And did they?'

'No — they didn't, so I asked them again and this time they went into a cubicle and shut the door. I thought at first "Oh well, so what". Then I thought this isn't good enough. I want to pee by myself. I want a certain privacy.'

'Oh Blimey.'

'So I opened the cubicle door. . .'

'What were they doing?'

'Snogging again — and I said "Out".'

'And?'

'They stood there and after a bit the boy said: "I love you! I love you!" (he put on a strong Hungarian accent for this). I said "Out!" and when he didn't move I took him by the shoulders and threw him out!'

'Did he resist?'

'No I think he was a bit surprised. But I mean to say — they've got machine-guns all over the country and yet in the lavatories — I don't know, perhaps it's a good thing, shows a degree of freedom of some sort, but bloody hell, fancy taking a girl to a men's lavatory for a snog — I mean a *lavatory*, where people go to — you know, I mean it's *awful*. What do you think he says to his girl-friend: "Fancy coming down to the lavatory for a bit?" It's disgusting.'

The thing that impressed me most about this ludicrous incident was that Harry was prepared to go to such lengths to have a private pee. Once the couple had withdrawn to a closed cubicle I'm sure I would have left them to it. In fact I would simply have gone to a cubicle myself probably rather than interrupt them or provoke an embarrassing confrontation.

The thing that impressed Harry most was that the boy had taken a girl to a lavatory. 'That's them by the way,' he said to me as we laughed over his story. I saw a boy of not more than fifteen or sixteen. He was also laughing with some friends and had his arm round a pretty, smiling girl of the same sort of age. They didn't look at us and the whole group was quite unconcerned, but a moment later the manager told them to leave.

I stayed in the buffet to write while Harry went for a look around, but he soon came back saying there was an open air pop concert going on so we went to look. It turned out to be a Youth Peace Club Concert. Euro lads and lasses sang folk songs and some tiny children sang *Brown girl in the ring* in enchanting English. They also sang *Swing low sweet chariot*.

Some of the singers weren't bad and more youngsters in jeans and T-shirts stood and listened, some with their arms twined around each other provoking Harry into making remarks such as: 'I suppose they are off to the lavatory,' or 'Hullo darling, fancy nipping down to the loo?!'

Youth Peace Club concert   Pécs

171

Peco listening to peace songs
Brown Girl in the Ring

The crowd listening to the music could have been from anywhere. The jeans, T-shirts, hair styles, jackets and behaviour were unplaceable. Only the few soldiers in their khaki uniforms looked Hungarian. They were only conscripts having a night out; they were not on duty.

On the way to the concert we saw an armed military policeman on

Pécs

patrol with an officer. His Kalashnikov was slung butt upwards across his back and the officer was dressing down two nervous-looking conscripts who were standing to attention while their papers were examined.

'Why on earth is he carrying that bloody great gun?' I asked.

'It's a kind of warning I suppose. It's to terrify — you could say it's a kind of terrorism.'

'When did a Hungarian soldier last fire on one of his fellow-citizens? It's unnecessary and very unpleasant.'

We drifted away from the crowd around the musicians down a pretty little street of shops. All the buildings were very old and charming. It was almost like a Hollywood set of the kind Danny Kaye used to prance down in musicals set vaguely in central Europe; a fantasy reinforced by the music floating through the still air. But this wasn't a set — real people were passing up and down and idly window-shopping. From a bar came the sound of talk and laughter and we stopped to drink some Hungarian apricot brandy made from barack. The little Büfé sold food and coffee as well as alcohol and two small children were playing by the open door. Outside the light was just beginning to fade. This peculiarly European way of promenading and taking refreshment and talking is something I miss in England. It's not the same as going to a pub or going out to dinner. There is some sort of relationship between European people and their streets and cafés that we English do not have.

Saturday 18 May

Before leaving Pécs we tried once more to do some shopping for our families. This time down the narrow pretty street we'd found yesterday. Here we had discovered two antique shops that had looked promising but one was closed and the other was full of rubbish. There was some porcelain that Harry quite liked but not enough to buy it and I found a Russian Army dagger in its metal-tipped sheath that one of my boys would have loved but it was very expensive and my son had enough weapons already. What I really wanted to get him was yet another weapon of a kind. I felt sure he would like a Hungarian stock whip because it was almost the same thing as carried by one of his film heroes and Harry had told me he'd once bought one in Hungary.

We asked the lady in the antique shop and were directed somewhere, from whence we were redirected and so on. At last a very convincing shopkeeper said we must drive thirty kilometres to Harony, south of Pécs, where there was a leather goods stall and there we'd find what we wanted.

As we had plenty of time before our 4.00 rendezvous with Papp Mária,

Restaurant
in Pécs

we went to Harony through the hilly, wooded and very pretty country-side.

Harony turned out to be quite a bit bigger than we'd expected so Harry began asking people the way. In the end a stout, elderly man got into the car and not only showed us the way, but after I'd bought exactly what I'd been looking for he invited us back to his house for a glass of wine.

We never learnt his name but he told us quite a bit about his life. He was about sixty I guessed, with an enormous pot belly. He wore a small square moustache and had thick grey hair. His eyes bulged behind his spectacles. He was like the cartoon stereotype German used by cartoon-ists just before the First World War. He was extremely friendly and courteous and had a way of talking that convinced one of his honesty. He lived in a spotless house set in a tidy garden and his smiling wife had a startling row of shining metal teeth.

He was born in Hungary but his father, who belonged to the German minority here, now lived in Germany with another son. Both our host and his wife spoke excellent German.

Over a bottle of his excellent white wine he told us that he often went to the West to visit his family but would not like to live there. Over there people worked too hard and were only concerned about their own welfare. There were more goods in the shops but he could get everything he needed here. A brother who lived in Austria came to visit him at least twice a year and might retire to Hungary where he was born.

When he was nineteen years old in 1945 the Russians took him to work laying oil pipe-lines somewhere in the Urals. He was not a prisoner-of-war because he was not in the army, he was just taken along with many other young men and women to work.

They did not get much to eat for the first two years and the winters were bitterly cold. They worked in 40 degrees of frost. But the Russians were quite kind and they had quilted jackets and boots for the winter. Nevertheless some prisoners died.

After two years the food improved and they got paid a little more. With their money they could buy clothes and some food. Many times he said to the Russians: 'I want to go home,' and they said 'Soon, soon'. He chuckled at the memory and Harry spoke the words in Russian at which the old man laughed out loud and said 'Ja! ja!' He was given work in a carpenter's shop which meant he could work indoors during winter which made life easier.

They had an eight-hour day and a six-day week. They had the official Russian holidays and could hope for some medical treatment. He had suffered from malaria and was sent to a sanatorium and cured, and given several days off to complete his recovery. There were women in the camp

177

as well as men and some Russian prisoners too.

One or two Hungarians had tried to escape but it was pointless, the distances were too great. They were always brought back. The punishment for trying to escape was not severe.

After nearly five years of this life he and the rest of the Hungarian prisoners were put on a train back to their own country. The Russian prisoners stayed where they were. The train carried them to a station somewhere in the north of Hungary and they were each given 20 forints (worth perhaps £5 in those days) and told 'You are free'.

I said to him: 'Your family must have been very, very pleased to see you.'

'When I got home I found that all my family had gone from Harony, except for an aunt who took me in.'

We were listening to this story sitting in our host's kitchen which was spotlessly clean and well furnished. The style was a little loud for my taste, bright flowery curtains, orange and yellow tiles on part of the wall, and on the door that led to a bathroom and lavatory two little figures had been fixed, one of a female child sitting on a potty and one of a small boy peeing. The wine was excellent and the welcome we received was as kind and warmhearted as it possibly could be. The gentleman's wife, who did not sit with us but was going about attending to household chores, called her husband out of the room and he heaved himself out of his chair to go to her.

When he returned he said dismissively that his wife was worried. She was made extemely anxious by these two strange men who had come from nowhere and were plying her husband with so many questions. One of them was even taking notes on what he was saying. Why was he being so foolhardy?

Harry earnestly begged the man to put his wife's mind at ease explaining again who we were and telling him that for us to hear a story such as his was a rare and fascinating experience. He waved his hand gently to and fro as if brushing Harry's words aside.

'I am telling you of my own personal fate,' he said smiling and unconcerned. 'There can be no harm in that. I have told her not to be worried.'

'Is it forbidden to talk to foreigners?' asked Harry.

'I don't know whether it is forbidden or not,' he replied.

Harry said: 'Everyone from the West can come here. They can see what life looks like; they can see what is in the shops and what is in the streets. But they come in their cars and cannot look into people's hearts.'

The Hungarian smiled and nodded and agreed that it is only by talking that that became possible.

Soon after this the man's son came in. He was about twenty-five to thirty years old and very suspicious. I think his mother had sent for him. He was unwilling to shake hands at first, but I offered him mine so insistently that he more or less had to. He kissed his father on both cheeks and they talked very briefly and then he left apparently reassured.

Before we left the old man gave us a bottle of his wine and his wife came out to say goodbye and she shook hands, so I think she was feeling OK by then.

Harry said as we drove away that it was not surprising that she had been worried. After all there had been a time not so long ago when meetings with westerners were expressly forbidden and would have resulted in unpleasant punishments. He also said that it was interesting that the man had said that he didn't know whether it was forbidden or not. The State never issued a statement about it, and thus left the people in a curious state of suspended anxiety. It is this uncertainty as much as anything else that produces the permanent whiff of fear that clings round the whole of Eastern Europe and so unnecessarily pollutes the life of the people.

We came rather suddenly on a large military lorry stopped bang in the middle of the country road. Its offside front wheel was just over the white centre line and two soldiers were standing by the vehicle and seemed to be repairing it. Harry was forced to come to a stop and peer very cautiously round the thing in order to pass it. One of the soldiers looked to see if any traffic was coming but made no signal to us.

'Our first Russians,' said Harry.

'So they are,' I said as we slowly edged past them and I saw their uniforms more closely.

We looked at them with lively interest and they stared back with such stony lack of expression it almost amounted to a threat.

'Typical,' said Harry. 'They make no effort to pull off the road.'

'You'd think they'd at least wave us on,' I said.

'No you wouldn't — not if you knew them.'

I wondered whether to stop and draw them but somehow I thought they might not like that too much.

'We must be passing a camp,' said Harry, indicating another Russian soldier walking along beside the road.

These were the only Russians we saw in Hungary although everyone we'd asked had told us that there were plenty around. Only one man expressed any direct dislike of their being in his country. Most people mentioned Russians quite casually, including the elderly man who had been taken away to the work camp.

We turned in at Mária's Agricultural Combine almost exactly at 4.00 p.m. The lanes leading to her house were more crowded than they

179

were last time we were here. Saturday afternoon was a time for sitting around and strolling. Some children were fishing in the river, and almost all the gardens were being worked over.

Mária was squatting by a fire under some trees that grew near her house. Over the fire was suspended a big black iron pot. She got to her feet and opened the gate calling to Harry to drive in. Elizabeth came out to say hello and so did her daughter we'd met last time. Mária's eldest daughter was also there. She was wearing a red track suit. The others were dressed as before except that Mária was wearing a vaguely khaki dress made of thick cotton which had a military look. Over it she wore a little white apron.

We were asked in after shaking hands and once more entered the little kitchen. From the other end of the porch Mária's neighbour watched us through the open door. She nodded but did not speak.

Beyond Mária's garden her other neighbours were busy in the hot sunshine and the horrible Alsatian guard dog neurotically moved about on the end of its chain.

We had chosen some presents for the family and Harry reached into a bag and produced the first one. I had noticed what a crude and inefficient tin-opener Mária had used to open the paprika paste and so we'd got her a very good Italian tin-and-bottle-opener combined.

She reacted quite strongly putting up her hands and almost frowning and demonstrating that this was an embarrassment to her. Harry gave it to her nevertheless and she took it. However her reaction had been strong enough to make Harry pause and he said: 'We'll try the other things later.'

We sat down and almost at once the big iron pot was brought in and a bowl of pasta was also put on the table. To drink we were offered lemonade because, said Mária, 'I couldn't give you wine as you are driving.'

The two daughters sat outside in the garden and Elizabeth sometimes sat with them and later joined us. Occasionally one of the puppies was shooed away from the door and the toddler from next door looked in. Only Mária sat with us.

She gestured to us to help ourselves. In the pot was fish soup. Four or five carp's heads looked gloomily up at us from the reddish liquid.

'Do we eat the heads?' asked Harry.

'I don't,' I said.

The soup was very good and very, very hot. It was almost solid chilli. It was the sort of hot that makes your nose run and your eyes water. I never know why the sensation of eating very hot food is so pleasant. Somehow I feel it shouldn't be, but it is.

I liked the soup very much and took a second helping later, and so did

Harry although later he told me it was so hot he couldn't really taste anything.

The conversation was very general and my notes on it convey, I hope, its casual rambling shape.

Harry kept translating for me and now and then I spoke to Mária through him.

Harry asked whether she had satisfied the curiosity of her neighbours about our first visit. She said: 'No, they haven't asked. When I first came here they never stopped asking me questions. I said to them "Ask me as many questions as I ask you". ' As she showed no interest in their private lives at all they got the message.

She thought the German Hungarian's wife had nothing to be afraid of now because of talking to foreigners, and she thought the story of the young couple in the loo was very funny. She was also amused by the story of us stopping the man attacking his wife, but also expressed strong disapproval of the man's behaviour.

'I would let no man beat *me* up,' she declared.

We scarcely talked about politics at all. Harry did ask jokingly whether Elizabeth could ask the authorities to lift her three-year travel ban. 'Perhaps if you asked very nicely,' he said.

Elizabeth smiled. 'I don't think so,' she said.

'Perhaps after the elections in June there'd be a new Government,' said Harry. Both women said firmly that that wouldn't happen and they didn't want it to happen. I don't think they picked up the banter and irony behind Harry's remarks.

Elizabeth said that had she over-spent her time by a year instead of two months she'd have been classified as a dissident and gone to prison.

After lunch we had coffee. The atmosphere had become very relaxed and comfortable. Harry's Hungarian seemed to improve moment to moment. He fetched his Hungarian/Russian dictionary to help when he got stuck, and felt he could risk giving out the presents.

He put the two parcels on the table, one for Mária containing a little bottle of eau-de-Cologne and for Elizabeth a bar of La Roche soap. We'd also brought a small chain necklet for Mária's daughter. They didn't pick up the parcels and expressed the same embarrassment as before.

Mária spoke; 'I did not ask you to come and have fish soup in order to get presents,' she said.

We protested that we knew that perfectly well and that these trifles were merely to express our thanks for her hospitality. In our country people often took little gifts for their hosts. It was a custom.

Reassured Mária opened her parcel. She said presents were very important to Hungarians. She picked up a glass dish from the table and said: 'This was a present.'

When she saw what she had got she turned her head away and put her hand to her mouth saying: 'Oh!' Then she leant forward, took Harry by the shoulders and kissed him firmly on both cheeks. She asked Harry for the English words and came round the table to me. 'Thank you,' she said and kissed me too. She looked pleased and we felt that the embarrassment over being given a present was gone.

Elizabeth also kissed us and said 'Thank you'. I watched Harry through the window go into the garden and give the little chain to the girl. She too protested but then accepted it and as he walked back indoors she opened the packet and showed the chain to her sister. We gave the toddler a Mars bar and he and his sister shared it.

Harry explained to Mária that I was taking notes because I was going to write about Hungary in my newspaper. Mária was very interested. 'Send me a copy of what you write,' she said. 'And put in my name.' Harry was so delighted by this response and its total indifference to possible official disapproval that he laughed out loud and cried out 'What a marvellous reply,' and in his enthusiasm he kissed her on the cheek. She laughed, possibly a little surprised by his gesture. He was completely taken with her remark and repeated it to himself in Hungarian and tried different translations.

She asked about my newspaper and I fetched a copy of a book of my cartoons and inscribed it for her. Harry tried to explain some of the cartoons to her and she and Elizabeth laughed and pointed. Her daughters came and took the book into the garden and sat with their legs dangling into an empty concrete paddling pool and looked at it.

Mária brought out a sort of magazine, with photocopied pages crudely stapled together, and showed it to us. It was produced on the Combine, and was a sort of light-hearted and vulgar satire on life here. The cartoons were scatalogical and bawdy and quite funny. She inscribed it with much love to her two British guests and signed it Márike and wrote her sister's name too.

Mária said she had dreams of travelling all round the world. She looked through the window down the garden at her neighbours. 'It is the end of the world here,' she said. 'When I was a child I read books about travel. I imagined myself in the jungle.' There was something sad about these childhood dreams which seemed pretty unlikely to come true. But she did not become maudlin; on the contrary she said optimistically: 'I'm planning for it. First I must find another job and get out of here.'

She told her daughter to put on a tape of Beatles' music. The familiar songs sounded strange in this setting.

The time came when we had to leave. Mária took my notebook and wrote her name and address and wagged her finger at Harry telling him I must be sure to send a copy of the newspaper. I glanced at the address to

182

make sure I could read it and she took the book back from me and wrote it again in bold capitals.

We shook hands and thanked her very much and her daughters came over to say goodbye.

As we drove away down the bumpy dirt road her neighbours stared at us with frank curiosity. Mária and Elizabeth stood in the road waving. We also waved until we reached a corner and looking back for the last time I saw them in the distance each with one arm raised, not waving any more.

It was easy enough to describe to each other the parts of this happy afternoon that had been particularly pleasing or interesting but what on earth had they made of us? We had no idea — and no way of telling.

I hoped Mária would find a better job and travel round the world and walk through a jungle. She gave us both the impression that she was a strong and resourceful person. Her whole personality was extremely attractive and if anyone deserved a lucky break she did. But the more of her fellow-workers we passed on the track the more sombre my mood became. They were not a very exciting looking lot and, like poor people everywhere, most of them, and probably Mária too, would not get far from this place. But she had a better chance than the others I felt sure and I hope she makes it.

I rang home twice and got no reply. I remembered the family were going sailing and hoped everything had gone OK.

Sunday 19 May

Harry contacted Éva who said that the friend she'd mentioned who could tell us more about Hungarian politics could meet us at 10.0a.m. We checked out of the hotel, and met Éva and István by the car.

István was a drama teacher and spoke very good English. He had a rather precise, almost schoolmastery, manner and although he laughed readily he gave the impression that life for him was serious. He did not describe himself as a dissident: 'I am not that important. They still let me travel.' But his fundamental opposition to the Government was immediately obvious and he was actively opposed to the system. His opposition had absolutely nothing to do with violence or any kind of behaviour that wouldn't be considered perfectly normal and innocuous in the West.

He explained that the opposition was in no sense a party, neither did it have any leadership, but it existed nevertheless. They held meetings, produced samizdat publications, and recently, because of the elections due in June, made numerous attempts to get opposition people nominated as parliamentary candidates.

183

The opposition, such as it was, was not even united. There was a Reformist wing who believed there were limits to political change — for instance, that it was unrealistic to hope to ever expel Russians from Hungary. They sought to negotiate with the Government in an informal way. An effort was made to change official reflexes and to try to influence decisions.

A larger part of the opposition thought differently. István belonged to this group. He said: 'We are optimists who believe that the history of freedom in Europe is not a lost cause.' I felt for a moment listening to him as if I had a direct line to the liberal reformers of 1848 and that István was continuing the work of Hertzen and could have been a friend of Turgenev.

He believed that personal contacts with people across borders undermined the authority of officials at home. It was particularly important for western writers to be talked to.

'Someone must speak out. Sometimes it is unbearable to remain silent. It is important to give people the impression that it is possible to actually SAY what everybody knows to be true. It is like the story of the Emperor's new clothes.'

He went on to say that he personally believed it was essential to improve the cultural life of the country because a well-educated, cultured people was more difficult to control.

The opposition was found mainly in Budapest and was not widely spread through the country, although he said that it depended a bit what you meant by dissident.

'You see there are many people who would say we should have an opposition who would defend the rights of the dissidents up to a point. Even people in the party. They will read samizdat publications and so on. But they will also say that the dissidents are wrong and miniature and misled. To understand this you must grasp the meaning of the word Doublethink. It was brilliant of Orwell to describe this phenomenon so well.' I understood István to mean that such people salved their consciences with liberal thoughts and even talk, but saved their skins by always toeing the party line when it mattered. These opposed attitudes do not alternate but co-exist.

Harry asked whether the Russians interfered much in internal matters. István answered that the relationship was not that of Lord and Master,.but Russia did not allow her children to quarrel (he meant both internally and between satellite nations). The satellites know what was possible and what was not and kept a 'smiling face' for the Russians. A kind of self censorship operates.

He said he had been told a ridiculous slovak joke. There is a slovak word 'Bača' (pronounced Bat-cha) which means a shepherd, the kind of poor simple man who lives up on the hills with his flock. The joke is: 'What do you get when you cross a gorilla with a bača?' and the answer is 'Gorbachev!'

He told us about a friend of his whose passport was withheld as a punishment for some infringement of the law. When officials were rung up and protests made on the grounds that it was illegal to take passports away as a punishment the reaction was: 'This does not happen in Hungary; what you are complaining about is impossible.' István laughed. He said: 'I like to actually touch the absurd centre of things like that. It is like an Ionesco play.'

I asked him to tell me about the elections planned for June. He smiled and said: 'That's a big subject — *what* about them?'

'Well for a start, why hold them?'

'That's what we ask ourselves and the truth is we don't know.'

He went on to say that there had been certain moves of a liberalizing kind in the early eighties. This was followed by a crack down and now perhaps they were interested in pretending that things were becoming more liberal again.

He made it quite plain, as Éva had done two days before, that the 'elections' were a complete sham. There were many, many attempts, some spontaneous, some organized, to get truly independent candidates elected but all failed.

All prospective candidates had to sign the programme of the Patriotic Popular Front three days before the election procedure. The Patriotic Popular Front was one of three names that the Party went by. The other two were 'The Party' and 'The Parliament'. They were all the same thing but three names gave the illusion of a variety of views. This programme or manifesto was three typed pages of what appeared to be rather vague declarations of intentions rather than a list of explicit goals.

At each constituency there were two selection meetings held and each candidate had to get a certain percentage of the entire vote. When a genuine independent managed to scrape through the first meeting the second was rigged to get him replaced. This was done either by simply miscounting the votes or by packing the place with obedient party members. These groups organized by the workers militia got to the meetings hours early and the public was denied access. Crowds of people gathered outside the rooms where meetings were held but their votes were deemed invalid. There were more of these independents than the Government had expected and sometimes a degree of intimidation was used against them, but usually the thing could be fixed quite easily.

All prospective candidates made speeches. The Government suppor-ters droned on about toeing the party line and peace, etc. Opposition candidates spoke about local issues and on such subjects as pensions for the less well off, the need to liberalize the laws about conscientious objection to National Service, matters concerning the Hungarian minorities who live in nearby Romania and Czechoslovakia and Yugoslavia, industrial pollution and racial prejudice against gypsies. Speakers also attacked the way candidates were being chosen for this election. They were told to complain to the official organizers. Their appeals were held in rooms packed with workers militiamen, and the ordinary public as usual were kept out. All appellants eventually received an identical statement saying the appeal was rejected.

I asked how could it be if all this was true and widely known that our original informant about the elections could have given us such a preposterously misleading version of them.

István's answer was 'Perhaps to make himself feel better. He feels more comfortable if he pretends to a foreigner that it's a true and fair election. It's maybe hard for him to admit frankly that his country is going in for such a gigantic fraud. It's a bit of doublethink.' He added: 'For some people it's made easier, I mean those for whom communism itself is a straight consequence of humane principles. For them it's very hard to imagine a non-Communist being good. For them whatever the Party does is all right.'

This conversation was held quite openly in a hotel coffee bar. We talked in ordinary not lowered voices and both Éva and and István obviously felt quite relaxed about answering our questions and didn't mind me taking notes. From time to time Éva queried something István said and once he quite good-naturedly laughed at one of her interjections and called her naive. She smiled and pulled a face and shrugged.

Before we parted István said: 'One theory about why the Party is holding these elections is that they, and perhaps more importantly the Soviet Union, are aware that in the West it is widely believed that life in Hungary is freer and generally more pleasant for all citizens than anywhere else in the Eastern Bloc. The Soviets think this is very good P.R. They are staging these 'elections' for consumption in the West not because they will make the slightest difference to life here.' Of all the reasons I was given for holding the elections this is the one that sounded most plausible.

CZECHO-SLOVAKIA

Monday 20 May

Before we left for Czechoslovakia Harry made one or two phone calls. One friend gave him a long shopping list of things that were unavailable in Prague. It was an ominous sign. The list included a golf cap and some car-seat covers and bits and pieces of equipment and household things. Harry said: 'It's always like this when I go to Czechoslovakia — it's not like Hungary.' He sketched in for me a picture of a much more repressive and strict regime. Czechs were not allowed to travel anything like as freely as Hungarians and there were currency regulations that made Austrians and other westerners unlikely to drop in as they could to Budapest. Across the Hungarian–Austrian border there was what they call 'local border traffic', but the Czech Government preferred to keep tighter control.

István had told us in Budapest that he considered that all contacts with the West undermined the authority of the Government, and the Czechs obviously agreed with him. This difference was noticeable when we crossed the border. We were the only car going through either way. It's true we had chosen a small crossing-point, but even so the roads were completely empty for many kilometres either side of the border.

The border guards were quite friendly. Harry spoke Russian to them and said their Russian was good.

They searched the car in a casual sort of way, asking us to open a couple of bags and taking a cursory look inside the car as well. One guard was puzzled by my occupation. It was down on my visa as artist. The czech word 'artiste' means something different and he asked politely if I worked for a circus. Harry laughed and he looked a little disconcerted. I showed him a sketch book of drawings I'd done in Hungary and he smiled and said 'Da da!'

As you passed from Austria into Czechoslovakia the change in the countryside and villages was unmistakable. Everything had a ragged and unkempt look. The edges of the road were rougher, the buildings oddly untidy and crumbling. It was almost as if the Austrians had made a special effort to ensure that their side of the border looked as good as possible and the Czechs had deliberately allowed their side to deteriorate.

The other difference was the appearance of mindless slogans on buildings and special constructions beside or even spanning the road. 'Peace, socialism and eternal friendship with the USSR.' 'If you build up our country you are strengthening Peace.' 'United with the Soviet Union for ever and ever.' We wondered who wrote these slogans. Did someone sit in a room chewing the end of his pencil trying to come up with a new one or did spontaneous workers' meetings produce them and send them off to a special centre for vetting and possible publication?

I once asked a Russian in Moscow what he thought about the slogans plastered all over his city and he looked at me mystified. 'What slogans?' he said.

'Those slogans,' I replied pointing.

'Oh *those* slogans,' he said as if seeing them for the first time. He peered at the one I had indicated and just shrugged.

The first sight of Prague when you approached the city by autobahn from the south was appalling. In the late afternoon light, which was dimmed by low clouds, we saw stretching right across the horizon a great wall of high-rise blocks arranged higgledy-piggledy over the rough ground like a giant's tank trap. As we broke through this barrier into the inner suburbs the streets became marginally less horrible but even there an awful grim seediness had settled over everything. I felt pretty rotten myself and I was only driving through. Then, as if we'd slipped many years through time, we emerged suddenly into a city so different that the shock almost made me gasp. On either side were noble buildings with majestic towers and turrets, beautifully decorated walls and windows, statues and touches of shining gilt. We glimpsed leafy squares and tiny alleys with arched entrances and with equal suddenness we turned down an ordinary little street and pulled up at our ugly modern hotel.

I immediately wished that we were staying somewhere else but actually we'd been lucky to find rooms at all, or so we were told, because Prague's hotels were already very full.

As we went in several car-loads of Russian Army officers in uniform drew up and entered with us. One fat officer with a gloomy unfriendly face leant on the reception desk near us as we checked in. Harry looked at him and counted his pips. 'He must be at least a colonel,' he muttered and walked over to him. The officer was considerably surprised to be accosted by a casually dressed, obviously western tourist carrying a

Grand Hotel - Border Town

violin case and speaking faultless Russian. I saw him shift slightly. He looked annoyed and vaguely uneasy. He said 'Da,' and Harry walked back to me grinning.

'What did you say to him?' I asked.

'I said, "Excuse me, I used to know something about Russian army uniforms, are you a colonel?" and he said "Da".' He laughed. 'I bet that's never happened to him before!' he said.

Because Harry was feeling tired we decided not to meet any of his friends but just to eat and get an early night.

In the restaurant we fell into conversation with a German-speaking Czech. Outside in the street a police siren began whooping. The Czech said: 'It could be an accident or a VIP.' We smiled and Harry said: 'Or better still a VIP who has had an accident!' and the Czech laughed out loud.

He began to tell us that travel to the West was getting very difficult these days. He used to go quite often but now he was told, 'You cannot go yet, it's time for others to have a turn.' Anyone going to the West was allowed 15 dollars per day each and children got 7.50 dollars. No one could really live on that unless they were going to stay with relatives or friends so everyone had to try to smuggle some hard currency out with them. If they were found with small amounts it was merely confiscated and they were allowed to go. But they might be questioned very closely on their return.

If they were found with large amounts of hard currency they were arrested at once and found themselves in a lot of trouble. For a start the police would want to know where they got the money from.

Harry said to me: 'This is a typical Communist trick. They make everyone into criminals and then they can pounce on them at any time.'

I asked: 'Why the present crack down?'

The Czech shrugged and answered: 'They want to raise morale.' I was about to ask more about this baffling reply when he noticed that I was taking notes. He said to Harry: 'Ask your friend not to take notes. I would rather he didn't do that where they can see it.' And he said to me in broken English: 'You are not in the free place now.'

I at once put away my notebook and pen and said I was sorry for being so stupid. But he waved aside my apologies.

'What would actually happen?' I asked Harry. 'What is he afraid they would do?'

'He is afraid that as he leaves here two men will step up to him and say: "What were you saying in there that was so interesting that your companion wrote it down?" '

'Oh Jesus!' I thought.

Soon afterwards the man got up, shook hands and went away.

Tuesday 21 May

I wanted to walk in the old centre of Prague to see for myself whether, as I have often been told, this was the most beautiful city in the world.

We took a tram across a bridge and got off when we thought we'd gone far enough.

We picked our way across some road repairs that seem to be going on permanently right across the Russian Empire, and looked around. No matter where my glance fell I saw a new delight. For the rest of the day this remained true. Prague was beautiful seen as a great panorama from the hills up by the castle, and down among its twisting streets and alleys were countless scenes of harmonious and enchanting details. We had stepped from our tram near Wenceslas Square, which you could say is a kind of Regent Street of the city. But to make any comparison such as that is to instantly mislead because Prague is an ancient city that has not been developed or as far as I could tell even repaired very much. The war did not destroy it and no greedy councillor or crazed architect had ever been allowed to play within its lovely centre. Therefore Wenceslas Square stretches its tree-lined length unspoilt all the way to the famous statue at its far end and is framed by the great gilt domed museum beyond.

The shops along its sides were well stocked — certainly the delicatessens seemed full enough. Harry bought some coffee because the coffee at the hotel this morning had been so foul. It was so awful that he made a scene and ordered some more. The waitress had told him that it was good coffee and later a waiter came and kept saying 'Mochaja! Mochaja!' Harry poured some out into his cup and pointed contemptuously to the pale brown stream.

'Coffee? Call that coffee? Looks more like weak tea. It is quite undrinkable.'

Tomorrow morning he intends to surprise the waiter by bringing his own coffee and telling him to use it generously.

The square was very busy with shoppers and once we saw a long queue outside a greengrocer's shop. We went in to see what was in short supply and it turned out to be apples.

Up by the museum we jay-walked across the road because we could not find a crossing and a young policeman looked disapprovingly at us.

The museum was closed and as we came out we saw the same policeman approach two girls. I couldn't make out what was happening. I thought the girls must be asking the way but they appeared to be showing him their papers.

'What's going on?' I said.

'He's probably fining them,' said Harry. I thought he was joking at first but then I began to think he was right.

'They were probably jay-walking like us,' he said, 'Let's go and pay their fine.' He walked over, took out his wallet and waved a note at the policeman. After a few moments he came back. The girls were German tourists who had crossed the road illegally. They did not have their passports on them and had no money with them and were getting slightly flustered.

'Were they grateful to you?' I asked.

'I think they were all so surprised they didn't know what to feel,' he said. The fine was about one pound each.

I had been given the address of a friend of a friend in a street near the

Wenceslas Square

castle and we took the metro in that direction. The metro was similar to the Moscow underground and extraordinarily clean and spacious compared with ours.

We came out in the Malstranské district where the streets were if anything more charming than where we'd been before. It's true that you could find dirty, empty streets but even there all the proportions of the buildings and the details of doorways and windows and dusty carved decorations were magnificent and the dirt even added to the romance.

My friend's friend was out, which was sad because the house was specially lovely. A lady nearby told us that the owner of the house would be out of Prague until next week.

We had lunch and went to see the collection of French nineteenth- and twentieth-century paintings at the Sternberk Palace. I always very much like the feeling it gives me to come across familiar paintings in unfamiliar places. I don't know why it should be so, but it's almost as if I am

sharing a joke with them — or that they are as surprised to see me as I am to see them.

There was an excellent collection of Impressionists and post-Impressionists, plus a tremendously good Lautrec, three superb Cézannes and an early Pissarro that I liked very much indeed.

I also whizzed round the exhibition of older European art and saw two Ter Borchs and a Rembrandt and a Lotto all of which were very fine.

I cannot convey the pleasure I got from walking back through the streets, past Kafka's house and across the Charles Bridge. It was rather like being in one of those dreams where everything turns out unbelievably well. You know that each turning will bring a new wonder and you are endlessly pausing for last looks before eagerly seeking the next delight.

I can't believe there is anywhere in Europe to compare with Prague.

As we found ourselves passing the United States Embassy we went in to see an exhibition of photographs and mementoes of the American troops in Czechoslovakia during the war. I tried to buy a little enamel badge of the American and Czech flags crossed but they'd sold out.

In the library were western newspapers on view and anyone could walk in freely and read them. I saw in the *New York Herald Tribune* that the Tories were now running third in the opinion polls!

Before returning to the hotel we bought some tickets for a concert of Smetana and Janáček on the Thursday evening.

We also entered a dirty scruffy-looking eating house where a few very ill-dressed and poor-looking men and women were eating horrible pink sausages and drinking beer and tea. We had stumbled on the lower depths. One or two men were playing slot machines which were American I think. On them was written: 'For extra bonus. . .' and 'Double pay out. . .' and so on.

That evening (Tuesday) we first drove to have drinks with some friends of Harry's for whom he had brought presents from Austria. They had asked for various odds and ends, including car-seat covers, soap, after-shave, and lacy tights. We visited two flats, both owned by comfortably-off citizens in a pleasant, quiet suburb. To come bearing such ordinary goods that were picked up and 'oooed' and 'ahed' over gave me a vivid picture of the difference between life here and in the free West. It was not just that we had these odds and ends in abundance but we could come and go carrying them any time we wanted to. The idea that our Government would be remotely interested in such activity was unthinkable. But here our hosts were watched and controlled and counted twenty-four hours a day from the moment they were born. In Hungary someone put it like this: 'They can give us things, but we have no rights.'

196

All the people we met were obviously extremely glad to see Harry, and not because he came with western goods. There was a happy excited mood and lots of laughter and eager talk in Russian and German (and English for me sometimes).

Later at dinner, along with much banter and chat, the conversation turned to politics. In Eastern Europe you could not avoid talking politics in one form or another because political power so invaded everyone's life.

One man said to me that a Swedish journalist had recently been granted an interview with a Government party official. The journalist had asked why there were so many restrictions on travel for Czech citizens. The official replied that there were no restrictions on travel, and that every citizen had the right to travel where and when he pleased. My companion closed his fist.

'This is just a lie,' he said.

'How do you know what the Swedish journalist said and what the official answered?' I asked.

'Because it was published in our papers,' he replied. 'Could you say in your paper that this is not true?' he went on.

'Yes of course I could,' I said. 'Furthermore, if I quoted officials unquestioningly like that in something I wrote, my editor would say I was a fool and that he would not print such misleading rubbish. He is not stupid.'

'It would be very good if you could say something about this,' said the Czech.

We heard the story of a man fired from a good position in the administration in 1968 because he'd been known to back Dubček. He had had to get a job driving a van that delivered meat. He now earned as much as a high-up Communist official because somehow or other he got the pick of the meat from the depot. He only carried the best and was paid extra by the people he delivered to. They got a commission on everything they sold. The more they sold the more they were paid so it was worth their while to bribe the driver who was now much richer than they were.

Harry asked whether, when the elderly leaders of the Politburo departed as death eventually knocked them off, there were younger men ready to take their places who might be more liberal or ready to change the present corrupt and authoritarian regime. The answer was: 'We don't know. We don't even know the name of a single one of the younger generation of leaders.'

It was noticeable that during this conversation, which took place in a small busy restaurant, the Czechs constantly dropped their voices or stopped speaking when waiters or other people walked near the table. I asked Harry to try to get them to tell us the latest political jokes that were going around. The answer was a smiling: 'Not here — perhaps you could come to my flat for such talk.' It was quite impossible not to get the impression that this system of Government literally forced people to break the law all the time. What this did to the general atmosphere of the country was very hard to know, but it must be extremely unhealthy, and a miserable way of running things.

Whether they were changing money on the black market, smuggling goods across the border, accepting or giving bribes, taking more than the official rate for something they were selling, whatever it was, in order to survive and provide for their families Czechs had to commit petty crimes.

Perhaps, as Harry surmised, it was all deliberate. A complicated ploy to keep the whole population anxious and uneasy and at the mercy of the prowling secret police.

The atmosphere in the streets and restaurants and art galleries was I think a bit misleading. For a start, many of the better-dressed cheerful-looking people you saw might have been visitors to the country. But, anyway, people do not go round looking gloomy and scared all the time.

Wednesday 22 May

When the waitress came to our table at breakfast-time Harry gave her half the coffee we'd bought yesterday and told her to find a large pot and make a strong brew. She was very amused at this order and smiled and shrugged and at once went off and returned very soon with a large jug. 'That'll do fine,' said Harry approvingly. The coffee was very good indeed and we gave the girl a 20-schilling note, (about 60p) so she was pleased too. The only one who wasn't pleased was the head waiter who came to give us our bill. He was the man who had quarrelled about the coffee yesterday morning. Even he tried to be less grumpy but I think he wanted a 20-schilling note too. But I didn't give him one.

Harry thought there was a racket in the kitchen — half the coffee that was supposed to go into the pots of the hotel guests finished up elsewhere. He was probably right.

By chance I noticed that Lidice was only 22 kilometres away from where we were and I suggested we visited the site. I could remember my father telling me about Lidice when I was a tiny boy. The story impressed me deeply at the time and had haunted me ever since. My father's face was very serious and sad while he told me about what had happened. I expect I had heard something on the wireless or seen something in a newspaper and asked him about it, otherwise it is unlikely that he would have told me so harrowing a tale.

On the way out of Prague we stopped at a Tuzex shop. This was a special sort of shop where western goods were on sale to all citizens. The only catch was that you needed Tuzex coupons to buy things with and you could only buy Tuzex coupons with hard currency. Usually it was illegal to come by hard currency but sometimes relatives or friends might send some or some dollars or marks might be acquired legally and then the treasures of Tuzex were yours, or as many of them as you could afford.

It was just like being in a Waitrose store in England. There were Kelloggs corn flakes and Fanta soft drinks and Nescafé and washing powders; and walking up and down the aisles were quite a few citizens doing their shopping in trolleys. There was even a counter where you could buy directly in hard currency which we did. I paid with dollars and got my change in dollars too.

Of course for anyone in the ruling class of a Communist State getting hard currency or in this case Tuzex coupons would not be a problem. These shops were therefore a sort of perk for the bosses, but ordinary citizens, if they had cheated well enough or if they had been very lucky, could make use of them.

To see the name Lidice on a signpost was a disturbing experience. I had always carried that name somewhere in my mind. The cool statement that this nightmare from my childhood was a real place and lay only 4 or 5 kilometres away down the road was a shock.

We missed the turning to the memorial, which was above the site of the original village and drove instead straight into modern Lidice, which was a well kept, even cheerful-looking place. The people in the streets were going about their business in an ordinary sort of way but I felt self-conscious, particularly when an old man looked up from cutting his lawn to watch a car with English number-plates drive by. He knew why we were there and I wondered if I was looking at a survivor.

It was upsetting that the memorial to Lidice and the site of the old village was not clearly marked out. The Nazis tried to wipe the place off the face of the earth as if it had never been, and succeeded, as any fool could have told them they would, in making sure its name would never be forgotten. But they were partly successful. You could no longer see where the houses stood and the streets ran. Now there was only an empty valley, dotted with clumps of trees where they once were, and dandelion clocks blowing in the wind.

I don't think the village should have been laid out and rebuilt as it was or even that the foundations should have been marked out, but somehow you should have been given a clearer idea of where you were and what you were looking at. If that could have been achieved then, in some tiny but symbolically important way, the Nazis' atrocious work would have been undone.

In the museum a film was being shown. It briefly described with the use of old newsreels the course of the war and the death of the ghastly Reinhart Heydrich. He appeared for a moment loping towards the camera in his black uniform, his face expressionless. The film included heartbreaking pictures of the village being blown up and burnt, and the bodies of the men scattered on the ground. Through the ruins of the innocent place Nazi officers picked their way looking with approval at a job well done.

To stirring music the film concluded with the destruction of the Third Reich. Dead Germans now littered the ground, Russian infantrymen waving the Red Flag ran up the steps of the Chancellery in Berlin and at last Lidice was rebuilt.

Elsewhere in the museum the story of Lidice was told again with still photographs and mementoes. The most chilling and in a way incompre-

Lidice

hensible exhibits were the various orders and requests for further information or instructions sent to and fro by the German authorities dealing with Lidice. The chatty almost casual style they adopted would be appropriate for describing, say, a drainage problem or the transport of some railway sleepers to another place. These documents were terrifying.

In a morbid and gloomy frame of mind we walked across the valley past a little garden donated by a Russian regiment which was dominated by an oddly cheap-looking wooden cross made from two pine logs. They might have been striving for simplicity but it looked mean.

The foundations of one house remained and could be seen and the position of the school was marked. A party of German schoolchildren aged about sixteen was being shown around. One was passing a carton of fruit juice to a friend and they were drinking as they walked by. The whole lot looked bored I thought. Some Czech children were also there, also just as fed up. They were larking about a bit too, no doubt enjoying a day off school.

We wondered how we would improve the place and invest it with more dignity. I came to the conclusion I would somehow make it much clearer where the old village had lain, and I would create one place

Remains of house
Lidice

specially neat and a garden or small park with carefully tended trees and flowers and if possible a piece of sculpture, and that would be the memorial.

I asked Harry if he knew whether after the war any survivors returned to Lidice. The children of that time would be our age now.

Back at the museum we asked the old lady who sold tickets about survivors. She told us 143 women had come back and 17 children. 'Everyone who came back', she went on, 'was given a new house here.' And she added: 'All the people who run this museum once lived in Old Lidice.'

'And you,' said Harry. 'Where did you come back from?'

'Ravensbrück,' she said. Another old lady was standing near the door. 'She was in Ravensbrück too.' Both women looked at us with expressions that were both sad and matter of fact; they had told their stories before and had seen the same helpless look on thousands of tourists' faces.

Outside the courtyard in front of the museum weeds were growing in the large cement flower pots and the decorative pond was empty, except for dust piling up in the corners. I had a sense of grief piled on grief and my emotions were shaken by useless anger. What was wrong with these people that they kept this place, of all places, looking so dead? When the old women were gone what would remain? Nothing but these cheap cracked stones and dented litter bins. There had been episodes in the history of the system under which this memorial was preserved, such as the show trials of the fifties, which were almost as brutal as the Nazis this place was intended to condemn.

As we were already out in the country we drove on to the nearby town of Klavno to look around and get some lunch. It was a large mining and industrial centre approached through a Dickensian townscape of smoking chimney stacks and huge factories. It also had the familiar outer ring of sprawling high-rise blocks built of grey cement and streaked with damp.

There was an old part of town with small nineteenth-century houses but it was all depressed, dirty and sad. We found a third-category restaurant and ordered beer and wienerschnitzel with salad. The waitress was an enormous woman of about thirty-eight, fully six foot tall, wearing a black mini-skirt and a frizzy hairstyle. Every time she went back to the counter from which she brought food, she took a swig of beer, and once drained a large tot of vodka as well. She never smiled or spoke but once she reached down and tugged gently at the moustache of a man who said something to her.

We might have been in a working man's café in England I suppose. The food wasn't that awful and the beer was good.

Before we left I started to draw the town hall that was decorated with a picture of Lenin holding up his fist. But it started to rain so I gave up. The streets were full of dull-looking people.

'They've given up,' said Harry.

'Poor devils, what else can they do?' I said.

On the autobahn a policeman stepped into the road and flagged us down but as we drew near and he saw the GB number-plates he hurriedly signalled us on.

'He's not really supposed to stop foreigners,' said Harry. 'Not unless he's got a bloody good reason.'

'Why was he stopping us?'

'Just to check, look at papers, ask where we're going, where we've been, keep us on our toes. . . .'

It was still raining when we got back to Prague and we parked the car at the hotel and took a taxi into town.

As we got in the driver said something in German and pointed at the meter.

He was saying that he was supposed to charge us a certain amount because he was a special hotel taxi, but that he was going to do us a good turn and only charge double what was on the meter. He had a complicated and completely spurious argument in favour of this plan and Harry leant forward with obvious pleasure to do battle with him.

First he ordered the driver to put the meter back to O as it was already reading the equivalent of £7 and said if that was not done at once he was going to get the director of the hotel and make a formal complaint. The driver began to produce bits of paper to prove his rights and Harry at

3rd Category Regiment
KLAVNO

once flung open the door of the still stationary car. The driver called him back but I think he already knew he was beaten. He kept saying: 'I am not a bandit.' He showed Harry a paper in Czech and to his horror Harry read it and said it proved nothing, it was merely permission to ply for trade at the hotel.

Soon the driver flung up his hands and turned the meter back and Harry smiled. 'He's saying pay me whatever you like — I'll take you for nothing,' he said. Harry hates taxi drivers trying to rook him.

When we arrived in Wenceslas Square we offered him either what was on the clock or a 20-schilling note. The man couldn't believe his luck for a moment, then said '20 schilling'. I gave him the note and as he took it he laughed and held out his hand to Harry as if to say: 'But if you were going to give me 20 schillings what was all that fuss about?' We shook hands all smiling and as Harry said: 'We parted friends.'

We had coffee and wrote postcards and later when the rain stopped we strolled again through the old town and back across the Charles Bridge. A mood of dreamy contentment came over me. From the bridge we

from Charles Bridge Prague

watched some swans scattered by a passing canoe beat their wings and run over the surface of the river before becoming airborne.

A wicked-looking girl asked us to change money. First she said she wanted hard currency for the Tuzex shop to buy cosmetics. Then she began to wheedle, saying that she needed to make money by these transactions in order to pay for her education.

I did a drawing from the Bridge while Harry fell into conversation with a charming Australian girl who was here visiting her Czech-born mother's relations.

Next Harry met a bunch of Russian drama students who were on a trip as part of their studies. They came from Leningrad and instantly began an animated conversation crowding round Harry and laughing. There were two men and three girls. They were mostly in their early twenties although one of the men whose name was Sergei looked a little older. In true Russian style he opened his bag and took out a bottle of vodka and we all had a slug.

'Aren't they wonderful?' said Harry. 'Let's take them for a drink.' There is almost nothing in the world he likes better than talking to Russians. He beamed at them and they smiled back. He was quite right — they were wonderful. Courteous and charming and full of enthusiasm and curiosity, they were marvellous companions. Some talked to me, pooling their English, asking me about the theatre in London.

We sat in a bar and they looked in my sketch-book. I did them a cartoon of Mrs Thatcher shaking hands with Mr Gorbachev, with the Red Flag and the Union Jack crossed behind them. They looked at it, chattering and laughing loudly. One of the girls asked: 'Could you draw a picture like that for your paper?'

'Of course.'

They asked Harry to describe my work to them and frowned and laughed at the same time as he explained the sort of freedom I had.

They asked if the politicians minded being caricatured.

Through Harry I told them that I had met Mrs Thatcher recently, and when I was introduced to her my companion had said: 'This is Mr Garland who draws the cartoons in *The Daily Telegraph*, perhaps you know his work,' and she had replied: 'Indeed I do, indeed I do,' with some emphasis and had shaken hands with a sort of good-humoured flourish as if to say: 'So you are that fellow.'

They were delighted and fascinated.

I told them about the days I had worked in the theatre and they asked particularly about Peter Brook and what he was doing these days.

Before we parted they gave us a little set of postcards that they all inscribed and as they shook hands said that if we were ever in Leningrad we must be sure to look them up.

Charles Bridge

Harry at his happiest – talking to Russians.

Harry remembered being in a hotel in Bulgaria. He had read the hotel rules, which were written up in several languages, and noticed to his surprise they did not say the same things. In English and French and German they were more or less similar but in Russian the time at which rooms had to be vacated on the day of departure was hours earlier and the notice went on to forbid the slaughtering and preparing of poultry in the hotel rooms.

'Time and again you meet Russians abroad and they are so awful you know at once why they require special notices in hotels. Then you meet a bunch like that and it is as if they are from another world. They are just marvellous,' he said. And they were very charming and friendly. We wondered where they were staying.

'Damn, I should have asked,' said Harry, 'Then we could meet again. Except I've found second meetings are often not so good as the first.'

'Do you mean as you get to know them they just turn into individuals like the rest of us?'

'No, it's more that a second set up meeting is different. If you meet by chance they feel free. If anyone wanted to know who they were talking to they could say: "We met by chance, it was impossible to be rude etc." But on a second meeting they feel more nervous. Sometimes they won't meet you a second time at all and if they do they have begun to think about possible unpleasant consequences, official disapproval, that sort of thing. . . .'

We had left the young Russians because Harry wanted me to meet a member of the ruling class in Czechoslovakia. He had in mind a trusted member of the Party, a scientific bureaucrat who had reached a position of considerable privilege and whose life was therefore quite different from the other Czechs we'd met so far. This man, who was once a colleague of Harry's at an international organization in Vienna, turned out to be away from Prague but his wife had accepted Harry's invitation to come for a drink.

'I knew this family quite well,' said Harry. 'They came to my house several times and I met their children and so on. But I'm surprised she agreed to come without her husband. I suppose when she's had time to think it over she may change her mind.'

He sketched in for me a few details of his ex-colleague's career. The man had proved his loyalty to the Party so many times that it was now beyond reasonable doubt. His reward was that he could work in the West travelling on a service passport which meant he did not experience time-consuming and humiliating waits at the border. His wife and children also had service passports and could come and go with him when he travelled on Government business. The fact that he worked in the West meant he could accumulate hard currency and that meant his standard of living shot up. Later a German who knew this Czech asked Harry: 'Is he still in Vienna? Good heavens, but what about his career, it's time he moved on isn't it?'

Harry replied that to a member of the Party this position could be seen as a career.

'He can travel in the West, he is rich, his position is secure . . . Why should he change anything.'

Harry was extremely interested to see if Stěpanka would meet us or not and when we arrived at our hotel lobby he said quietly: 'Ah, ha! There she is.'

Sitting by a window was a woman of about fifty, smoking a cigarette. Her hair was well cut and her dark suit was smart and fashionable. Round her neck was a loosely knotted silk scarf. If you passed her coming out of Liberty's in London you would not notice anything

212

particular about her. Here, in her own country, she looked foreign.

She spoke good English, learnt partly during the time she had lived in Washingon with her husband. With every other Czech I had met here and with all the Hungarians we had talked to the week before, politics and 'the system' were somehow included in every subject that was discussed. It didn't matter whether they were directly referred to or whether they were acknowledged only by an aside, a joke, or perhaps a lowered voice but you could not escape politics. But with this woman Stěpanka, married into the ruling class, the opposite rule applied. It would have been extremely embarrassing to refer to politics or the system or repression of any sort. Even questions about her country had to be carefully phrased so as to avoid criticism or disapproval.

First we argued about whether she was inviting us out for a drink and a bite or we were taking her. We won because we'd already booked a table in a wine cellar where Harry knew he could buy a wine that he particularly liked.

We sat in grand style in a modern hotel and Stěpanka talked about her children. The eldest was living in London and working for a travel agency, the two younger ones were with her in Prague. The question that was occupying her at the moment was which school to send her youngest daughter to in Vienna. She wanted the child educated in the West where she could learn a foreign language and benefit from a better education.

She could have been any affluent Westerner discussing the difficulties of educating children. I thought of her fellow-countrymen waiting and waiting for permission to make trips abroad; unlawfully collecting hard currency; then if they got permission having to risk smuggling the money over the border under the suspicious eyes of the armed guards. Harry's wife had an uncle who was stripped naked and thoroughly searched twice before he was allowed to cross into Austria recently. They were looking for his personal papers, birth certificate and so on, which would be a sure sign that he intended to defect. Stěpanka would expect no such indignity.

It is hard to describe the peculiar way in which her position affected the conversation. I felt as if I was conniving to a certain extent in the game she was making us play of pretending that she was an ordinary woman living in an ordinary country.

The conversation was easy enough but it was all about children and holidays and the weather and such things. We were drinking very good wine, and after two bottles and a couple of hours she mellowed a bit but there was no possibility of discussing more delicate subjects.

When we paid the bill I said to Harry: 'Shall I give the waiter 20 schillings?' I was still carrying a wad of these useful notes and liked to hand them out because they were so well received.

'Yeah, why not?' said Harry and under Stĕpanka's watchful eye I handed one over. The waiter smiled his thanks and Harry said with mock innocence to Stĕpanka: 'We've found people prefer a small tip in schillings over here.' She was obviously in a difficult position. This was something she must disapprove of but she also knew that to do so would make her look foolish.

She pretended at first not to know what Harry was talking about; she frowned slightly and tilted her head to one side as if puzzled then said: 'Oh! oh yes.' She smiled indulgently and said: 'Yes, yes, of course.' She might have been talking about disobedient children who had been caught staying up after bedtime or running outside in their slippers.

'Let's give one to the violinist as well,' I said. All evening he had been playing away and smiling. He was a young rather small, sad-looking man. As we walked past him Harry tucked a note into the side pocket of his jacket. The violinist continued to play but raised his eyebrows in thanks. Stĕpanka walked on and seemed not to notice.

Perhaps she didn't mind really because when we drove her home she invited us in for a coffee and cognac.

The flat was in a smart area and was large and well furnished. Nothing very grand in the way of pictures or antiques but full of odds and ends. Stĕpanka's family had recently acquired a huge and appalling young dog. It was about the size of a small horse with a great black mouth from which spit dribbled between its white fangs. It barked and jumped up, pushing its appalling face into one's trousers and bounding this way and that. I was glad to see that it went for it's mistress's knickers in the same crazed way. She pushed it aside laughing and scolding it. Every time it came near me I pointed at Harry and said: 'Kill'. He tried stroking it under its chin and his hand came away wet with dog spit. 'Oh God,' he said.

Stĕpanka turned on the huge TV and fetched coffee. On the screen half a dozen girls in peasant costume sang an unbelievably dreary song against a ludicrous painted backdrop.

Then the news came on. The main story was that the President had been re-elected. He was shown greeting and being greeted by squads of officials and their wives and inspecting a guard of honour.

'Was his re-election in any way a surprise?' asked Harry.

'Oh no,' said Stĕpanka with all seriousness, 'There was no other candidate.'

'Mm, a real cliffhanger,' murmured Harry, but Stĕpanka did not hear.

She told us what people were saying. 'These are workers in a factory — they are saying they are very pleased the President is re-elected because he is a good man.' This she reported quite seriously. I glanced at Harry; he was looking at the screen with a serious expression but he caught my eye and almost laughed.

'This man is a famous footballer,' said Stěpanka. On the screen a handsome man in a tracksuit talked earnestly into camera.

'Is he pleased too?' I asked.

'Yes, he is saying the President deserves another term because he has proved how excellently he fulfils his duties.'

It sounds absurd as I write it but she was absolutely serious and watched the screen closely as she spoke.

She told us how the President's wife had once driven up to her (Stěpanka's) country house while the family were all sitting in the garden. The first lady had missed her way and accepted a cup of coffee while she was given directions. It was not until she had left that a neighbour told Stěpanka who her visitor had been.

As the stony-faced old men on the TV screen went through their ludicrous rituals of hailing the newly 'elected' President, it was extremely difficult for me to believe that anyone could take such nonsense seriously for a moment. How could such dreadful old rascals get away with such a preposterous charade? They were nothing more than greedy old bullies and everyone knew it. It was a comic spectacle in a way and it made Harry and me laugh, but it was also distinctly unpleasant. We asked various Czechs later whether they had watched these celebrations on TV. The reaction was invariably laughter at the idea of anyone asking such a ridiculous question.

Before we left Stěpanka had one more surprise for us. I asked her what she suggested Harry and I do or see on our last day in Prague. She suggested visiting a castle some 20 kilometres outside the city and said she'd like to come with us. We thanked her very much and agreed to telephone her at 9.30 in the morning. Both of us felt this was not an ideal arrangement for our last day but it was hard to see how to avoid it. We said goodnight and went back to our hotel.

Thursday 23 May

Harry phoned Stěpanka at 9.30 a.m. as arranged and came back to where I was having breakfast with a big smile on his face.

'First the good news,' he said. 'The castle is open today. Now the bad news. Stěpanka can't come.' He laughed. ' I bet she rang her husband and he told her not to.'

'Did she say why she can't come?'

'Yes, she said she has an appointment at the doctor and she completely forgot about it.'

'I suppose she might have done.'

'Yes she might have done. Or she might have felt this has gone far enough; or her husband might have warned her off — we'll never know.'

'I'm glad anyway — she had a way of stifling conversation.'

'Yeah, I agree.'

The day was overcast and dull and we decided we'd drive out to the castle anyway and maybe stop in a village for lunch. But before we left Harry was keen to visit a museum that he'd seen listed in a guide book. It was called The National Security Corps and Interior Ministry Armed Forces Museum and we were interested to know what on earth it could contain.

It was in a large, exceptionally clean-looking building and in the foyer a soldier stood to attention with a shining bayonet fixed to his rifle.

Before we entered the museum proper a man asked us to slip canvas slippers over our shoes; then we paid our money and went in. It was the sort of place that at first stimulates jokes along the lines of 'Where do we pay to get out of here' and so on. But our mood quickly changed to something less facetious.

I rapidly became convinced that the whole place had a message and was itself a warning.

The museum consisted of many large rooms full of display cases and weapons with here and there huge, grotesquely ugly statues representing struggles and victories from the past. These exhibits told in chronological order the story of Czechoslovakia from the 1930s through to the present day with all emphasis given to violence, murder and crime. Not only the rooms given over to the Nazi occupation were ghastly, but right up to the present day horror upon horror was presented with truly awful bluntness. One of the exhibits from the Nazi period was a small guillotine complete with zinc bucket to catch the severed head and the gouts of blood. The bucket had three neat little holes for the blood to run out of. It was clear from the mechanism that two men were needed to work the machine, one to wind up the blade and the other to release it. Both men must have stood within inches of the victim. It was one of the most chilling and obscene things I've ever seen.

But to ram home the message, case after case contained photographs of murdered intelligence officers and the victims of crime and disorder. Dead bodies were shown freshly exhumed and rotting or floating in muddy ponds; some lay in topsy-turvy blood-stained rooms; some in quiet fields; all were evidence of what happened if law and order failed. Or to put it another way all showed what you could expect to happen should your Communist guardians be overthrown or attacked. Alongside this theme there was another, and that was how expert and irresistible the secret police were. There were display cases showing various technological developments in the hunt for criminals. Men and dogs were shown being trained; marksmen at practice and border security

216

being installed. The message here was: 'If you step out of line it is useless to try to escape or resist.'

Implicit in both these themes was the actual point that only the all-powerful and benign State stood between you and all this nightmarish brutality.

A photograph of Brezhnev and Husak inspecting a guard of security men was particularly unpleasant. Who knows what these security men would stop at to carry out the orders of such grim masters. On the day we crossed the border into West Germany and within a few kilometres of where we had been, two young Germans who had strayed over the border were shot at by Czech guards. One was hit in the leg. A German who told us about this incident said: 'They are very clever. You might think that the guards would say: "All right we have orders to fire but we cannot be made to hit." But they have tests. Only crack shots are chosen for this duty. If they fire and miss they can be asked: "How come you didn't hit that easy target." This can be difficult for them.'

Another profoundly disturbing exhibit was a hologram of a bust of Dzerzhinski and an accompanying case of photos and memorabilia about him. Dzerzhinski was the head of Cheka, the Russian security force in the twenties. He died suddenly in 1928 but not before he had made a name for himself as the most bloody and ferocious butcher of his time. I suppose Stalin himself, Hitler, Himmler and Heydrich and Pol Pot now challenge his fearful place in history. A statue of Dzerzhinski stands outside the Lubianka in Moscow.

As we left the museum several parties of schoolboys were arriving to visit the place. I felt it was no place for children. It was offensive and disgusting and the best thing to do would be to close it at once.

On the way out we bought postcards of the museum and a set of badges marked SNB, the initials of the security forces in Czechoslovakia. Harry pinned a badge on his jacket to see whether anyone would react to it but as far as we could tell no one did. I felt I did not want to wear the badge, even as a joke.

We drove to Karlstein in the afternoon. The countryside was quite pretty.

In the evening we had been invited for a little meal and a drink with some friends of Harry's before we went to a concert. We ate dumplings stuffed with plums and served with either poppy seed or curd sauce. When our hosts asked us what we had been doing today Harry flashed his SNB badge at them. They frowned and laughed at the same time, as people do when someone makes a risqué joke or tries a really bad pun. They agreed that the museum was intended to terrify and added that the system only continued because of continual pressure from and surveillance by a large strong police force. If this pressure was relaxed 1968 would happen all over again immediately. Peter, whose house we were in, said most people where he worked had two jobs, an official one and a more lucrative unofficial one. These unofficial jobs might be carried out not just in official hours but on official premises as well. The country only held together because people continually broke the law. I wondered aloud what would happen if a general work-to-rule was organized so that everyone only did what they were supposed to do. The idea appealed to Peter and he smiled: 'I think everything would soon come to a stop,' he said, and then went on 'but of course you could never organize it.'

One result of this general corruption was that if the police wanted to find something on someone it was no problem. 'Ninety-nine per cent of us do something unlawful,' said Peter. In case there should be any doubt I should add that Peter was an honest and intelligent man and in the West would certainly be a successful and law-abiding businessman. The system he was forced to live under was corrupt, not he.

At eight o'clock in the balmy twilight we went to the concert hall, a magnificent building with marble pillars, gilt and statues, to hear the Smetana Quartet play Smetana's Second String Quartet and Janáček's String Quartet known as Intimate Letters. There was also a work by a modern Czech composer called Eban.

This was rather a lot of Czech music for one night but it suited my tired and over-excited mind.

Later we walked for an hour or so through the old city. The beautiful streets were almost empty although the wine shops and bars were full and noisy. I felt terribly tired and light-headed but unwilling to leave this marvellous, romantic place. As always each corner and doorway and empty cobbled square was even more enticing than the one we'd just left. We could stop and stare, or retrace our steps or just go on deeper into the unknown. Invariably we'd find a new wonder; an arcade in deep shadow; a church front gleaming softly in the street lights; a fountain with a pretty statue; or just a house so perfectly proportioned that a sense of peace and order filled the mind with inexpressible contentment.

Finally exhaustion drove us home, but still unwilling to go I dawdled, half hoping we would not find the car too soon, and I lingered often to look back and paused to listen for footsteps, and voices calling in the damp night air.

Friday 24 May

We headed for the West German border, taking a somewhat roundabout route in order to visit Karlovy Vary (Karlsbad), where I hoped to find the past preserved as in Prague and feel the presence of Victorian and Edwardian tourists, perhaps even the shades of Turgenev or Chekhov.

But when we got there we were both disappointed. There were nineteenth-century terraced streets, but most of them so dirty and shabby that it was hard to see their former splendour. And anyway some Communist sprite has caused a high-rise hotel to be built right in the heart of the town, which dominated and ruined the prettiest part. This masterpiece of ugliness was huge, grey and shapeless and it had been festooned with slogans that exhorted the unfortunate Czechs to build yet more socialism and even closer ties with the USSR. The effect was indescribably offensive, the effrontery breathtaking.

Moving on we picked up a hitch-hiker. A cheerful student who told us he was studying engineering. He and Harry conversed in Russian. Among other things he said that he was going to tell us a military secret.

'I am learning to repair tanks,' he said.

'Tell him that if they are going to be used against us to make sure they don't work.'

The boy laughed and said he thought the world would be a better place without tanks.

'The army is for generals.' He also said that he just didn't believe, as he was taught, that there was the slightest military threat from Germany.

We asked whether any of his fellow-students belonged to the Party. He replied that of twenty-one students in his group only one had joined.

The only reason to join was to try to advance your career but it was not essential. You could get a good job without being a Party member.

He hoped to get permission to visit someone he knew in Vienna one day. If he did well in his exams he might be allowed to go to Hungary or Yugoslavia. We wished him luck. What stupidity to keep such an intelligent and impressive young man from travelling.

We dropped him off in Karlovy Vary where he showed us the way to a good restaurant. When we gave the waitress a 20-schilling note as we paid our bill she was so surprised and pleased that she curtsied.

We walked across the charming and picturesque square which looked like an illustration from an old German book of fairy tales. I did a couple of drawings and we took a few photographs.

'Let's go,' said Harry. 'This place is getting me down.' He didn't mean the little town or the square, he meant it was time to get back to the West. I felt the same. The drabness of the people's lives, the limits on their freedom, the invisible menace that hung over everything, the ugliness of the system, all had a depressing effect which could get quite overwhelming.

As we drove the last few kilometres towards the border I thought how ironical it was for us to be thirsting for the free air of Germany. Forty or so years ago we would not have raced so confidently towards that country.

At the check point we waited in a small queue. Drawn up alongside us was a lorry that appeared to be full of clay. Soldiers with dogs were examining it. One probed the whitish dusty load with a long iron spike, a sleek Alsatian dog clambered to and fro sniffing. We wondered what they were looking for.

'People probably,' said Harry.

Even though we were carrying nothing illegal I felt nervous. The guards were not offensive and politely asked us to empty the boot. They opened the spare wheel compartment and felt down the sides of the seats but they left our luggage and soon returned our passports and waved us forward.

A kilometre or so further on a German border guard leapt from a window and glanced at our passports.

'How do you like the car?' he said nodding at Harry's VW. They chatted about petrol consumption and acceleration for a few moments and we drove on.